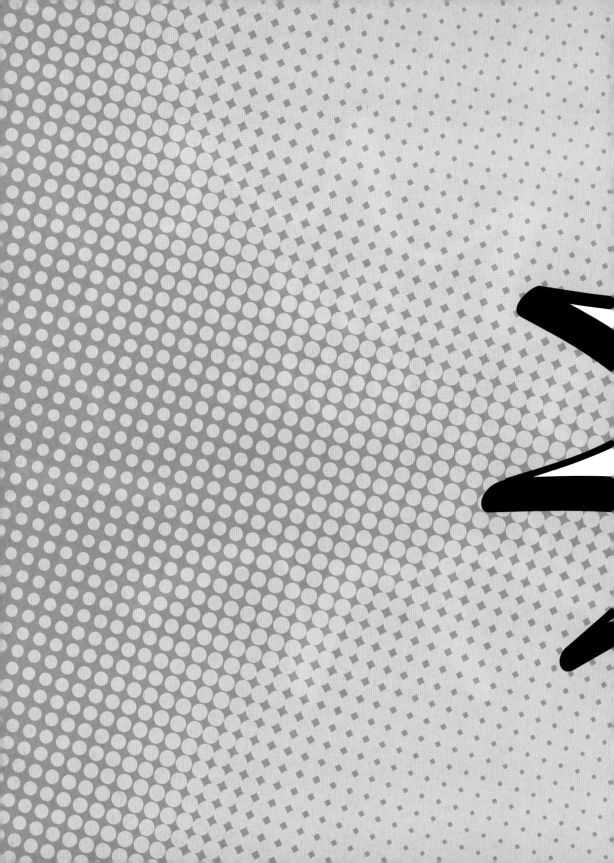

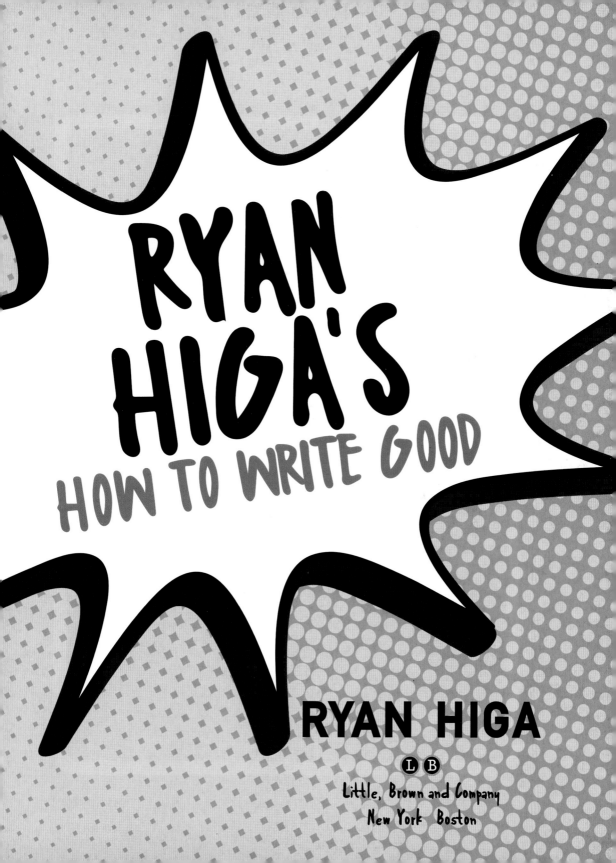

RYAN HIGA'S HOW TO WRITE GOOD

RYAN HIGA

LB

Little, Brown and Company

New York Boston

Copyright © 2017 by Higa TV Productions, LLC
Illustrations by John Nugroho

Cover photo by Howard Huang
Cover copyright © 2017 by Hachette Book Group, Inc.

Little, Brown and Company
Hachette Book Group
1290 Avenue of the Americas, New York, NY 10104
Visit us at LBYR.com

First Edition: May 2017

Little, Brown and Company is a division of Hachette Book Group, Inc. The Little, Brown name and logo are trademarks of Hachette Book Group, Inc.

The publisher is not responsible for websites (or their content) that are not owned by the publisher.

Photo on page 4: Howard Huang
Photo on page 15: Courtesy of the author

Library of Congress Control Number: 2017935291

ISBNs: 978-0-316-46407-9 (hardcover), 978-0-316-46406-2 (ebook), 978-0-316-56163-1 (Target)

Printed in the United States of America

WOR/CORAL

10 9 8 7 6 5 4 3 2 1

AUTHOR'S NOTE

Oh, that's me. The Author. I need to be official here. My editor told me I had to be. So, here goes:

This story recounts events from my life over fifteen years ago. I've told it as best as I remember it. Some names and identifying details have been changed. Oh, and some conversations are as good as I can recall them because who can remember word for word a conversation you had fifteen years ago?

Okay, now you're prepared to read on. So, go forth and read!

CONTENTS

Prologue. Prologue? My editor told me I might want to start with a prologue. Okay. But what the heck is a prologue?

Oh, of course! An event or action that leads to another event or situation.

Yeah, I Googled it, and I still don't know what it means, or how to write a proper one. So instead, let me just use this space in the book to introduce myself.

My name is Ryan Higa. You might know me from the Internet. But I am also the author of this book.

Actually, I shouldn't say "the author." Technically, I'm a coauthor of this book. You aren't supposed to know this, but my publisher—hereafter[1] to be known as The Publishing Company, or TPC for short—hired me a ghostwriter. A real, professional, anonymous writer who's supposed to secretly help me tell this story. Her name is Sarah, but we'll just call her by her last name, Tomlinson, to protect her identity. I've even included a picture of Tomlinson and me so you can have a better idea of who's going to be telling you this story.

---

[1] Whoa. I've barely even started my book and I've already started writing things like *hereafter.*

(She is a ghost, after all.)

Look, if it isn't blatantly obvious, I've never written a book before. I'm not gonna pretend like I'm a professional book writer. I'm not even gonna pretend that I read a lot of books. I'm not gonna pretend I say things like "going to" instead of "gonna." I'm not a good speeller. My grammer aren't not that good.

And with every word I write in this document that will become The Book, I get one step closer to cracking the teeth of the people who work at The Publishing Company, from all the cringing they'll be doing reading this.

So why am I writing a book?

A. Because I'm a YouTuber and I'm trying to become a bestselling author to get people to think I'm smarter than I really am.

B. Because I'm a YouTuber and that's what YouTubers do to make that cha-ching, bling-bling, $$$, etc.

C. Because I signed a contract with a publishing company thinking it would be a breeze to write a book, only later realizing that I have no idea how to write one.

D. Because I have a story to tell that I believe will help influence and inspire people (especially kids) who are going through tough times in their lives, to not only persevere through those tough times, but to excel in them.

Well, if you guessed D, you're absolutely wrong!

I'm a YouTuber trying to make dat money by tricking foos into thinking I'm smart, all while screwing over a publishing company that—

Okay, that was a joke. Not necessarily a great joke, but at least now I know that jokes don't translate the same way in a book as they do on video.[2]

The real answer is D…and, well, a little bit of C too.

---

[2] Look, Ma, I'm learning already! (Seriously, this book is so hard to write, my mom is helping too. So I know she's reading this. HI, MOM.)

So. This is the story of how I was thrown to the ground in middle school and called a Chink. This is the story of how I almost died. This is the story of how I learned the value of perspective, which is probably one of the only things we actually have power over in life.

This is also the story of how I learned to write a book. And you can too!

You see, if this were a YouTube video, I'd be completely confident that I could tell this story the way I want to. However, this is a book and I may or may not have contractually bit off a little more than I can chew.

And let me tell you…Books: They don't taste good…or is it "well"? Taste "well" or taste "good"?

And let me tell you…Books: They don't taste good…or is it "well"? Taste "well" or taste "good"?

Like I was saying, I may have bit off a little more than I can chew. And let me tell you…Books: They don't taste well….[3]

⬤　⬤　⬤

[3] It's pretty cool that TPC hired me an illustrator, though. This might actually be kinda fun.

Welcome to *Ryan Higa's How to Write Good,* by me, Ryan Higa, where you're going to learn how to write your own book from a college dropout who has never written a single book, who struggled in basic-level English classes throughout his life, and who doesn't know the difference between "your" and "you're." So, you know your in good hands!

Who is your main character? And where are you going to start his or her story? The first part of this is an easy one for me—*I'm* the main character.

But where should I start my story? That is a great question.

Anyway, where was I? Oh yeah, where to start the story. Just because this is the beginning of a book about my life doesn't mean it has to start at the beginning of my life.

(Trust me, you do not want to hear about that.)

Instead, let's meet our hero at oh, about age ten, in a moment that will help you understand where Young Ryan was in life, both literally and figuratively.

● ● ●

"I WANT TO QUIT!" I screamed.

Mom continued to drive me from basketball practice to judo practice without saying a word to me. We were already at that part of the car ride where she had stopped fighting back.

"It's not like I'm any good," I said. "I never even win!"

"I already told you, that's not the point, Ryan!" she replied, clearly frustrated.

We continued on in angry silence, as I began to focus and gather my composure. I knew I had one last shot to win this battle. It was risky, but it's all I had left. The Tri-Beam Offensive. A last-resort tactic I had developed over the years, in which I attack from three different angles: Sympathy, Health, and Education. It had a low success rate, but at this point I was desperate.

"It's not like I'm gonna get better anyway, plus I have a headache, and I have a lot of homework!" I said as I looked up at her with a purposely pathetic expression on my face.

Here it was, the moment of truth.

As I waited for her to respond, seconds felt like hours as we continued in the direction of my doom. I watched the palm-tree-lined Main Street pass by, with its red awnings over the storefronts of local businesses. It was only a five-minute drive through downtown Hilo from the gym where I had basketball practice on the outskirts of town to the county recreation facility where I had judo, but it was a welcome oasis between stuff I hated. I wished it would last forever. Or, usually I did. Maybe not tonight. She still hadn't said anything. She showed no signs of anger, but at the same time, why wasn't she saying anything? *How long has it been since I used the Tri-Beam? A minute? An hour? Have we traveled backward in time? This is torture!*

Suddenly she took a deep breath and slowly exhaled. "You're going," she said calmly.

You're going. That's how it always ended. Whether it was going to basketball practice, judo tournaments, or something school related, it didn't matter what argument or excuse I had. Once I heard those words, in that calm voice, I knew it was over.

I sank back into my seat, defeated. I stared out the window for the rest of the ride. When we pulled up to the dojo, I opened the door and rushed out of the car to avoid hearing the words that had haunted me since I was five years old and this judo torment began. And not just once a week either, but every Monday, Wednesday, and Friday night—plus Saturdays, if there wasn't a tournament with other judo clubs from around the island. But it was too late for me to escape from…the words of doom.

"Have a good practice!" my mom said with a smile.

I turned back and glared at her. She continued to smile, which only pissed me off even more. Not saying a word, I slammed the car door shut and trudged to the entrance of the dojo.

At ten years old, I already hated a lot of things in the world, and judo was at the top of the list. Maybe because I was horrible at it and got beat up a lot or because the Senseis (or "teachers," for those of you who don't speak French) treated us like animals. Perhaps I hated it because it was something that I was forced to do and not something I chose. Whatever the reason, judo practice was the closest thing to hell in my young mind.

I bowed at the entrance of the dojo (I hated it, yes, but I wasn't going to disrespect it intentionally) and entered to find that everyone was already lined up, about to begin. *Crap!* I thought as I started to run toward the changing room, hoping to go unnoticed. It was too late.

"Higa!" Sensei yelled.

Instantly, I stopped, stood up straight, and faced him.

"Hai!"[4] I answered.

Everyone turned to look at me. I could feel them all judging me. Looking at me as the terrible little brother of Kyle Higa, the naturally gifted judoka who was everything that I was not.

[4] Now, this isn't "hai" like, "Oh, hai, Internet. I can haz ur luv now?" It's more like, "HAI! This is serious judo business!"

"Get back over there and bow correctly!" he yelled. My Sensei was never not yelling, but he always had an extra note of disappointment in his yell when it was directed at me.

"Hai!" I yelled back as I ran to the dojo entrance.

I slowly bowed once again, this time making sure it was perfect: My legs were together, my feet were facing the right way, and my bow came down all ninety degrees. I finished the bow and looked around as everyone continued to watch me. I glared back at each of them, wanting so badly to scream, "WHAT THE HELL ARE YOU LOOKING AT!" when I was suddenly brought back to reality.

"Hello!?" Sensei yelled.

I instantly shifted my eyes back to him and straightened up again.

"Hurry up and go get changed!" he yelled.

"Hai!" I yelled as I sprinted off.

The other students' laughter faded as I made my way to the changing room. The two minutes of peace and quiet alone in the changing room was the best part of practice, yet it was already ruined.

All I could think about was hate.

How I hated judo.

How I hated my Senseis for yelling at me and embarrassing me.

How I hated the other students who never got yelled at.

How I hated my brother for saddling me with an expectation I could never live up to.

How I hated Mom and Dad for forcing me to be here.

How I hated everything about my life.

Like, *everything*.

● ● ●

It took ten years of living for me to ask myself for the first time, "If this is what life is like, wouldn't it be better to be dead?" This question led me to so many other questions:

But what if you die and go to hell and it's worse?

Does hell even exist?

I wonder if everyone else thinks about these things.

Is this how all ten-year-old boys feel about their lives?

But before I could even start to really think about the answers, I had another horrifying revelation....

It'd been more than two minutes....

"HIGA!" I heard Sensei yell from outside the changing room, even angrier than before.

"HAI!" I yelled as I sprinted out the door.

LESSON 2
WHERE DOES YOUR STORY TAKE PLACE?

When writing the beginning of your book, it's not enough to just introduce your main character. That would be like showing an action hero in front of a green screen without the city and the villains (which were probably added in later with CGI).[5] Show the reader where the main character lives. This can mean places, people, time. All of it sets the scene.

●　●　●

Here's the thing about my hometown of Hilo: It's pretty small. Although the Internet just told me that it's the biggest small town on the Big Island of Hawaii. (That's really what my island is called—the Big Island. Because it's the island of Hawaii, which is one of the eight main islands that make up the state of Hawaii.) Also,

[5] If you must know, this chapter was added later too. So was the line on page 16 about the palm trees I saw on the car ride. My editor told me I needed to add descriptions like that so you could "see" where I lived. She didn't like it when I said, "Can't my readers just Google Hilo if they're curious?"

because I'm 90 percent sure you just pronounced it wrong in your head, it's like *hee-low*, not *high-low*.

So, I grew up in a small town on a big island, and there was nothing to do there. I mean, I'm sure you're picturing us surfing and going to luaus every night, and eating poke, and doing other "Hawaiian" stuff like that. And yeah, we did have nice, sandy beaches. But to get to the nice, sandy beaches, where the older kids liked to go and hang out and surf, it meant an hour-and-a-half drive. And as a kid, I had no way to get to the beach. Plus, I was happier at home playing video games anyway.

So I pretty much hated Hilo. And while I got along well with my parents, I hated being the baby of the family. My brother, Kyle, was four years older and was supercompetitive with me basically from day one, and that pretty much set the course of our relationship. (What kind of big brother is competitive with A BABY?! *My* big brother, I assume.) And as I got older, I hated anything that took me away from what I liked to do (watching movies, playing video games, riding my bike).

But I didn't get any say about that. I was always being told how I had to spend every minute of every day. And so I hated that too.

Since I hated pretty much everything around me, there was no escape. I was trapped and powerless. And, you guessed it, I hated that too. Year by year, these feelings added up, until all the hatred and anger became one big, bad, dark thought.

● ● ●

So, there you have it. Setting set. Let's move on, shall we?

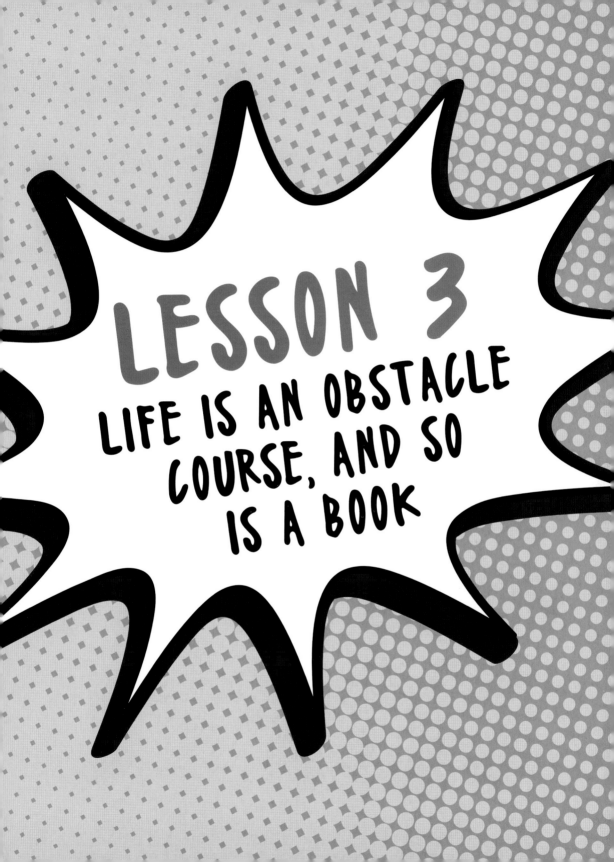

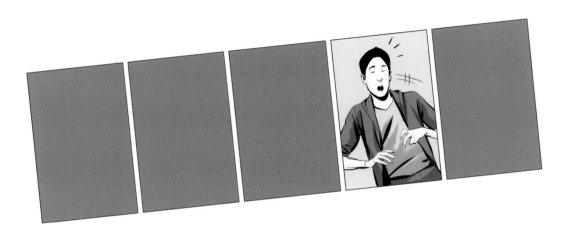

Okay, time to get the story moving by establishing a little bit more who your main character is and where he or she is at in life. And then throwing in an obstacle: The Conflict. For example, we now know that ten-year-old Ryan is an over-dramatic, whiny kid who hates everything about his life and has no idea how easy he really has it.

●　●　●

Hmmm, what do I want? What do I want!? I thought.

PlayStation 2? No, think bigger. I want…to grow up to be a rich and famous actor? No, that's not even realistic, I'm Asian! Damn it, what do I want?

I could tell by everyone's faces that I was taking way too long to make a wish.

My parents and friends were all gathered around to wish me a happy birthday, and there I was, unable to decide what to wish for. The candle wax was about to drip down onto the cake.

Okay, I need to hurry! Maybe I can wish for Nicole from school to feel the way I feel about her? No, that would be a waste! Love is never affected by wishes, according to that one Disney movie. What was that movie again? I asked myself.

Suddenly, one of the guys interrupted and snapped me back to reality.

"Hurry up! You're gonna be twelve by the time you blow out the candles," he joked, causing everyone, including me, to laugh.

I took a deep breath and blew out all the candles on my cake, only to realize that I had never actually picked a wish.

PLAYSTATION 2! I yelled in my head.

I was too late. We opened all the gifts and there was not a PlayStation 2 in sight. It wasn't a big deal. I was never one of those kids who got really excited over gifts. I was more excited about all my friends from school being allowed to sleep over since school was out.

Usually, my friends and I were hyped for summer and wished it would last as long as possible. This summer was a little different. Fifth grade was over, we were done with elementary school, and we all couldn't stop talking about how great middle school was going to be! A fresh start in a new environment where you finally begin establishing a different hierarchy of coolness. We had plans to take specific classes together, change our look with new clothes and haircuts, etc. This was the first time any of us were truly looking forward to school starting. It was gonna be awesome…or so I thought. My gigantic bubble of excitement was about to get popped.[6]

[6] Fun fact: This is called foreshadowing. It's when you give a hint of what's going to happen next, but you don't reveal everything, so the reader feels all nervous and excited and just has to keep going. We'll stop at nothing to make you keep reading! (Insert maniacal laugh.) (Ugh, books are so hard to add sound effects to!)

…or so I thought. My gigantic bubble of excitement was about to get SO popped. "IT'S NOT FAIR!" I cried.

Mom had just explained to me that she wouldn't be registering me at the middle school all my friends were going to. Instead, she'd signed me up for a charter school that had opened downtown. Even though it was a public school, I could only enroll if they had an opening—and just my luck, they did.

"Kyle didn't have to go to a stupid charter school!" I said.

"If I knew how bad the teachers at his school were back then, he would've gone somewhere else," Mom said.

Mom was on the Parent-Teacher Association board for three years while Kyle was at the middle school ALL MY FRIENDS WERE GOING TO. According to her, a handful of teachers there were against making changes to improve the school. So there was no way she was sending me there if she didn't have to.

"I won't even know anyone at the charter school!"

"Ardie is going there too," she said.

"I don't even like Ardie!" I replied without hesitation.

She gave me a look as if to say, "Really." She knew I didn't mean that. Ardie wasn't necessarily my closest friend, but he was definitely someone I enjoyed hanging out with. He was one of the guys on my basketball team, so I'd seen him three to four times a week, every week, since we were five.

"Is it too late to switch the—"

Mom cut me off.

"Ryan…" she said calmly.

I already knew what was coming. It was over. No need to even bother with the Tri-Beam Offensive.

"You're going." She stared at me, giving me that look you give a dog that keeps begging for a treat.

Knowing that saying anything back to her at this point would not only be futile but risky, I clenched my fists, turned around, and stomped toward my room. I was so frustrated and angry. Each step I took got harder and harder as I made my way to my room. I wanted to break the tile beneath me. Punch a hole in the wall. Slam my door so hard that it broke off its hinges.

But I didn't. I just sat on my bed, in silence, feeling completely helpless.

There was nothing I could do about it. It wasn't just about me changing schools. Every time I got this upset and felt like there was injustice, all the things in my life that I considered to be unfair came flowing back to me simultaneously.

I'd go down a whole stream of things I hated and thought were unfair, from something as big as being forced to move to a new school to something as small as not being able to choose which channel we watched after dinner.

Maybe that's what I should've wished for on my eleventh birthday: death. But is that what I really want?

About a month after Young Ryan's mom broke the news to him that he wasn't going to the same middle school as his friends, and popped his bubble of excitement, Young Ryan finally accepted that he was going to this new charter school. You see, learning to accept things that are out of your control is one of the greatest things Young Ryan would learn that year. His entire attitude toward moving schools shifted from complete pessimism to being open and optimistic!

I'm not going. She'll have to break open my door and drag me there. I'm not going to that stupid fake school, I thought as I stared at my locked bedroom door.

I heard her footsteps coming down the hallway, getting closer and closer. My mom was a tiny person, but I'll never forget the sound of her walking toward my room to make sure I was awake. Every time I heard it, it was like that scene in *Jurassic Park* where they hear the T. rex stomping and see the glass of water shaking more and more. It was only a matter of time before the T. rex would show up and let out a horrifying, ear-piercing roar.

"Ryan! Time to wake up!" Mom said in her annoyingly happy and upbeat morning voice. She knocked on my door a few times too. I ignored her.

I didn't have much of a plan. All I knew was that if Mom was going to force me to go to this dumb school, I wasn't going to make it easy on her. If she wanted me to go to that school, she was going to have to drag me there.

"Ryan Higa! Get up!" she said cheerfully as she knocked again.

There's nothing worse than a cheerful person in the morning when you're in a terrible mood. But I stayed strong. I was willing to hole up in my room and endure her annoying cheerfulness as long as it took, just to piss her off and make her feel the same anger and frustration I felt.

"Better hurry up, your Hot Pockets are getting cold," she said as she went back to the kitchen.

Damn it. My weakness. I should've seen that coming.

Well played, Mother. Well played, I thought as I opened the door.

I walked into the kitchen and noticed that something looked different. It was still dark outside. I looked over at the clock on the stove.

"Six thirty? Why'd you wake me up so early?"

"Your new school starts a little earlier," she said.

"What time?" I asked.

"Seven thirty."

Great. Yet another thing to add to the list of why this school is the worst.

It took about fifteen minutes more than usual to get to school, because this new school was located in downtown Hilo, which was a lot farther than my old school (and what I wished was my new school). A lot of people think of downtown Hilo as this beautifully historic and well-preserved place. The way I saw downtown Hilo? An old, dirty, run-down bunch of buildings that reeked of piss from all the homeless people who stayed there.

BUT IT'S STILL A WONDERFUL PLACE TO VISIT, WITH TONS OF ACTIVITIES AND A COLLECTION OF WONDERFUL, UNIQUE, LOCALLY RUN BUSINESSES THAT CAN'T BE FOUND ANYWHERE ELSE IN THE WORLD!!!
—PAID FOR BY THE HAWAII TOURISM BUREAU

"Have a good day! I'll be back at two thirty to pick you up for basketball," Mom said.

"Two thirty!? This school starts earlier and ends later too!?"

"Yup!" Mom smiled and nodded.

I slammed the door shut and she drove off, leaving me in a sea of strangers. I looked up at the building, and it was exactly as I expected: old and dirty. A homeless man was sleeping in front of a vacant shop right next door. It looked less like a school and more like a place where a secret sweatshop might be hidden.

How had this become my life? And how was I going to survive it?

"SEA OF STRANGERS" IS PRETTY GOOD, RIGHT?

IT DOES HAVE SOME NICE ALLITERATION.

A LITTER WHAT?

NEVER MIND. IF YOU STOP TO PAT YOURSELF ON THE BACK AFTER EVERY NICE TURN OF PHRASE,

YOU'RE NEVER GOING TO FINISH THIS BOOK.

OKAY, HOW ABOUT I KEEP WRITING AND YOU PAT ME ON THE BACK. DIVIDE AND CONQUER!

YOU ARE A UNIQUE INDIVIDUAL, AREN'T YOU?

AHA! YOU DO SPEAK SARCASM.

KNEW IT.

I DO. I JUST CHOOSE TO USE IT SPARINGLY.

LIKE HOT SAUCE.

WHAT? NOW YOU'RE NOT MAKING ANY SENSE.

WHAT'S THAT, LIKE, MERCHANDISING?

HEAR ME OUT. YOU AND I BOTH KNOW THIS IS THE PART OF YOUR STORY THAT REALLY GETS INTERESTING.

BY MAKING THIS CHOICE FOR YOU, YOUR MOM SET YOUR LIFE ON A DIFFERENT PATH.

AND (SPOILER ALERT) IT DEFINITELY WASN'T FUN TO LIVE THROUGH.

YOU CAN SAY THAT AGAIN.

IT DEFINITELY WASN'T FUN TO LIVE THROUGH...AND THIS IS THE PART OF THE STORY THAT GETS DARK. DURING THE SERIOUS PARTS OF A BOOK, A LITTLE SARCASM GOES A LONG WAY.

WHY? BECAUSE HUMOR CAN BE A WAY TO KEEP PEOPLE AT BAY,

WHEN YOU DON'T WANT THEM TO SEE HOW MUCH SOMETHING HURTS YOU.

YEAH, THAT'S WHY IT'S AWESOME!

AGREED. BUT THIS IS EXACTLY THE PART OF THE BOOK...

...WHERE WE WANT TO INVITE THE READER TO GET CLOSER,

SO THEY CAN REALLY FEEL WHAT YOU WERE GOING THROUGH.

MAYBE EVEN RELATE TO IT BECAUSE OF SOMETHING THEY'RE GOING THROUGH IN THEIR OWN LIFE.

OH, RIGHT, THE WHOLE POINT OF THE BOOK.

HEAVY.

YEAH, BUT I KNOW YOU'LL MAKE IT ENTERTAINING TOO.

BECAUSE I'M A GIVER.....

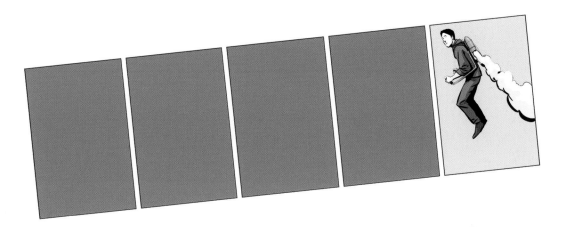

In order to deal with the conflict, the main character needs a little help along the way. And he's going to encounter some resistance, usually in the form of an enemy or an archnemesis, or both. Meanwhile, the assistance can come in many forms—the parent, the coach, the sidekick, the best friend, the love interest. Overall, these helpers and hurters are known as the supporting characters, and while most of them are introduced within the first few chapters (like you've already met my mom and heard about my brother), they can also pop up throughout the book. Like so.

●　　●　　●

I started walking toward my doom, a.k.a. the entrance of my new school, when I heard someone call out my name from behind me. I turned around to see that it was Ardie, who was just getting dropped off.

"Sup!" I said to him as he caught up to me.

We walked in together. Ardie hadn't been a particularly close friend in the past, yet I don't think I've ever been happier to see someone I knew. We fell in with the other students and made our way down to what seemed like a cafeteria.

"This doesn't even look like a school," Ardie said.

"I know, where are all the classrooms?" I said back.

When we reached the cafeteria, we sat down at one of the open tables, observing all the other kids.

"Plenty of haoles here, huh?"[7] Ardie said, laughing.

I looked around, and Ardie was right. It was like white-people central. There must have been at least a hundred people in that cafeteria, and I couldn't spot more than one or two other Asians. Ardie was half white, so even he didn't look Asian. This was the first time I'd ever felt like a minority in my eleven years living in Hawaii (which was my entire life).

"OKAY! Quiet down, everybody!" an older white man yelled out to us.

He had long white hair and a white beard and mustache. He kind of looked like a stereotypical Santa, except he was wearing tan khaki shorts, brown sandals, and a white shirt with a faded logo that looked like it'd been used about two years longer than it should have been.

Maybe a retired Santa?

"If everyone could gather around here," the older man said.

"I think that's the principal," Ardie said.

"I don't think so, look at what he's wearing," I said.

Everything got quiet as we all formed a semicircle around this Santa-looking man.

"Welcome to Charter World Charter School. I am your principal, Mr. Santa!"

---

[7] Okay, in this case, I'm **99.9** percent sure you've pronounced this wrong in your head, and I don't want you to be an embarrassment to yourself, so say it with me: *howlies.*

• • •

Okay, obviously that wasn't his real name,[8] I completely forgot what it was. But in my mind he really did look like a retired Santa, so that's what I'll call him.

• • •

Mr. Santa explained that instead of separating us by grade, we'd be divided into six different groupings, based on how well we did on a placement test we were about to take.

"Wow. Test on the first day? Bullshit!" one of the students shouted. He was tall and dark, with boy-band hair. He must have been older, because he looked like he'd been shaving for years.

A bunch of the students next to the boy-band kid laughed.

"Watch your language," Mr. Santa said in a very unmerry tone, glaring at the boy-band kid.

It was clear that this jolly old man had a scary side to him. He pointed at a chart of the groups and told us that whoever was in our group would be our classmates, in every class, for the rest of the year.

As we waited to start the test, a feeling of anxiety suddenly swept over me. I began to overthink, as I've always had a tendency to do.

What if I forget how to do math? I haven't done math all summer! What if I forget how to spell? Oh my God, I'm gonna fail my first test!

---

[8] That's not my school's real name either. Gotta keep some details to myself in this whole deal. And I'm having a lot of fun giving out fake names. You get a fake name and you get a fake name and you get a fake name!

●　●　●

Now, I know Young Ryan is sounding like a little drama queen. All that anxiety and negative thinking over a simple placement test? Well, unless you grew up with the mentality that your grades are the most important thing in your life, as well as an extreme source of pride—or shame—for your parents, it's difficult to understand. My parents may not have had accents, but they were pretty much Asian stereotypes when it came to school performance and grades.

The traditional American grading scale looks like:
A stands for Excellent.
B stands for Good.
C stands for Average.
D stands for Poor.
F stands for Failure.

This is what the stereotypical Asian parent grading scale looks like:
A stands for Average.
B stands for Better try harder.
C stands for Care for an ass whooping?
D stands for Don't come home.
F stands for Forgiveness…as in, Forgive me, for I have murdered my child.

So yeah. This placement test may not have directly affected Young Ryan's grades, but failing a test, regardless of what it's for, is unacceptable. Of course he was stressed.

• • •

Although I had no confidence in how I performed overall, I felt surprisingly happy. This was one of the first times in my life that I enjoyed taking a test.

"That was so stupid, huh?" Ardie asked me.

"Totally!" I said back to him, hiding the fact that I kind of enjoyed it. I mean, a lot of it had been pretty basic math and reading-comprehension stuff—

And then, with ten minutes to go, I realized I still had at least three pages left and started to panic. But as I turned the page, I saw it had nothing but a few words on it:

Extra Credit: Answer the following questions to the best of your ability. Good luck!

I expected to see some crazy equations that I'd never seen before. I was wrong.

There were no equations, just a bunch of confusing word-problem riddles from top to bottom. What did these riddles have to do with education?

It didn't matter. I had less than ten minutes to answer as many as I could, so I got started right away.

Extra Credit #1: *Two fathers and their two sons go fishing together. They each catch one fish to take home with them. They do not lose any fish, yet when they arrive at home they only have three fish. Why?*
ANSWER: ///

Extra Credit #2: *What five-letter word becomes shorter when you add two more letters to it?*
ANSWER: //

Extra Credit #3: *You have two buckets. One holds exactly five gallons and the other, three gallons. Assuming you have unlimited water and there are no measurement markings on the buckets, how can you measure exactly four gallons of water into the five-gallon bucket?*
ANSWER: //

I didn't even know if I got the extra-credit answers right, but I'd never had an opportunity to think in such a different way before. It was actually kind of fun!

● ● ●

As you can see, I covered the answers that Young Ryan wrote down with a special ink, so that you all could try figuring them out on your own if you want.

If you don't want to attempt to figure them out on your own, just hold the book up to a light source, such as a lamp, a ceiling light, or even the flashlight on your cell phone, and the answers will magically appear.

I'm sorry.

Here are the real answers that Young Ryan wrote down:

Extra Credit #1: *ANSWER: There are only three people: a grand-father, his son, and his grandson.*

Extra Credit #2: *ANSWER: The word* short. *Add the two letters* e *and* r *and it's* shorter.

Extra Credit #3: *ANSWER:*
1. Fill the five-gallon bucket.
2. Pour it into the three-gallon bucket, leaving two gallons.
3. Empty out the three-gallon bucket.
4. Pour the two gallons in the five-gallon bucket into the three-gallon bucket.
5. Fill the five-gallon bucket and pour it into the three-gallon bucket until it's full, leaving four gallons in the five-gallon bucket.

Speaking of wanting people to like me, this is probably a good time to officially introduce my elementary school love interest, Nicole, who I casually mentioned earlier. She was definitely right up there in the cast of characters of my young life and definitely someone who I wanted to like me.

● ● ●

Nicole and I met when we were in second grade. She was the most beautiful vision of perfection I had ever seen. She had this long, cascading dark hair. Like a river.

And these brown eyes that sparkled. Like, um, brown gemstones.

I'd never met anyone like her before.
And I loved her.
I just knew it: She was the girl for me.

Actually, Nicole was just a normal little Asian girl, but I only saw her through my eyes of love, which were maybe exaggerated. Her eyes were definitely not exaggerated when she looked at me, though. Not that she ever did look at me.

AW, SHE MISSED OUT!

THANKS, TOMLINSON. I KNOW YOU HAVE TO SAY THAT, BUT I STILL APPRECIATE IT.

BY THE WAY, WHAT ENDED UP HAPPENING WITH THE TEST?

NOTHING THAT ENDED WELL FOR ME.

OH, SORRY. SPOILER ALERT.

Writing a book is sort of like peeling an onion.

Okay, so, books have layers. Once we establish the basics of our story—who the main character is, where he lives, what he wants, who's around him—we also have to make sure we dig deeper, and show another degree of significance or meaning. That's where backstory comes in. It's information from the hero's past, sometimes told in flashback or revealed in dialogue or narration, that helps the reader understand how the hero came to be who he is and what strengths (and weaknesses) he's working with.

Extra points if the writer pauses to explore a character's backstory just when the reader really wants to know what's going to happen next in the present-day story. So let's just say our hero has taken a big, major, scary test that's going to determine the fate of his entire future...and the reader *really* wants to know how he scored and what it all means....That's the perfect moment to build suspense by pulling away from the action for a chapter of backstory.

9 A simile is a literary device writers use to compare a thing to some other thing that seems pretty different from the first thing to help readers understand the thing. Like, say, writing a book is like peeling an onion. This is different from a metaphor, BTW, which also compares two things but never uses *like* or *as*.

• • •

When I was five years old, I had a realization that formed the basis of my personal philosophy for, well, pretty much the rest of my existence so far:

Life's not fair.

I have to give at least some credit to my big brother, who was nine at the time. Not only was Kyle better than me at everything—all challenges and competitions, video games, and *of course* judo.

"Ouch!"

Kyle had this thing about pinching me.

So, one night after he did it as I walked by him on the way to my room, I decided that the only proper, FAIR retribution was for me to pinch him back. But then he just pinched me again. Of course, then I had to pinch *him* again....

Oh, and by "one night" I mean ALL THE TIME.

We could really go on like that forever. Except he always found a way to get in the last pinch.

Even at five years old, I knew it was all rigged. And by "it," I mean *life*.

AGAIN WITH THE NEGATIVITY?

I THINK THAT'S JUST HOW HE IS...

WE THOUGHT HE WAS FUNNY.

WHERE IS HIS FUNNY?

WE'VE GOT TO START DOING MORE RESEARCH ON PEOPLE BEFORE WE LET THEM PUBLISH A WHOLE BOOK FULL OF WHATEVER CRAZY IDEAS THEY HAVE ABOUT LIFE.

WELL, TO BE FAIR TO RYAN—

JUST SEE WHAT YOU CAN DO TO MAKE IT A LITTLE MORE POSITIVE.

Just take a typical day in my life in kindergarten. I mean, what could go wrong in kindergarten? Don't eat the paste and you'll be fine, right?

It didn't go down quite like that for me. See, there we were, doing our whole kindergarten thing, when the teacher said, "Okay, class, everyone please sit criss-cross-applesauce."

I didn't want to sit crisscross-applesauce. I was perfectly happy where I was in my little kindergarten-sized chair. As my classmates moaned at the instructions, I realized I wasn't the only one. But as we all grudgingly sat down on the floor and began to fold our legs, I turned to my right and…wait, what was this? One of the girls was sitting on the floor *without* her legs crossed. And our teacher was smiling at her. Mind you, as I well knew, this girl—let's call her Mary Sue—had a prosthetic leg. But I didn't care about a minor detail like that. It was no excuse. Our teacher had said "*everyone*." Such an exception to the rule wasn't fair.

And when something wasn't fair, it made me mad. So mad that there was no way I was going to just sit there, CRISSCROSS-APPLESAUCE, when I didn't feel like it, and keep my righteous anger to myself.

I stood up.

"Ryan?" our teacher said. "Is something wrong?"

I didn't hesitate. Five-year-old me was a spitfire. "How come she doesn't have to sit cross-legged like everyone else?" I fumed, pointing at Mary Sue, who, now that I think about it, looked as if she wanted to dissolve into the ugly beige carpet.

"It's difficult for her to sit cross-legged," our teacher said, smiling back and forth between Mary Sue and me, trying to keep the peace.

The other kids squirmed, but nobody came to my defense. I was in this fight alone.

"But you said *everyone* had to sit crisscross-applesauce," I reminded her.

She took a deep breath before saying, "You're right. Everyone except Mary Sue."

"Well then, that's not *everyone*, is it?" I said.

"No, Ryan, it's not. But that's how it is."

After that, our kindergarten teacher was always very careful with her words around me. She didn't say "everyone" unless she *really* meant "everyone."[10]

What I didn't know at the time was that this outburst—and, okay, others like it—prompted my teacher to have an extra-long parent-teacher conference with my mom that year. We're talking a double session.[11]

After detailing some of my class disruptions to my mom, my teacher broke it down like this:

"Ryan is basically like an old man in a little kid's body. We're all going to have to be patient with him, because it's going to take some time for his age, and his grade level, to catch up with his analytical mind and his keen sense of justice. So we'll probably see more outbursts like this for a while."

That made sense to my mom since, you know, she knew me pretty well. They agreed that I hadn't done anything that required punishment. They were just going to keep an eye on me as I tried to change the system, wherever and whenever I thought it needed overhauling.

●　　●　　●

Of course, I didn't know any of this back then.

All I knew at five years old was that much of my life seemed unfair, and I had very little control over any of it. And I did *not* like not having control.

You see, that was the age when my parents started enforcing this rule they had in our family: I *had* to do a martial art, and I *had* to do a team sport....

---

[10] Wow, thinking back on this story just taught me something else about myself: I was a total word guy. Still am. It's like nails on a chalkboard when I hear someone use a word incorrectly or not mean what they say. And look at that! I used a simile. I might be qualified to write this book after all.

[11] Sorry, Mom!

●   ●   ●

Judo is not one of the more popular martial arts, like karate or tae kwon do. But judo is what my older brother had been doing (and excelling at) since he was five. So my parents decided that's what I'd do too.

Here's the thing: When you first start learning judo, it's fun. You learn different postures and footwork and ways to fall. But after you start getting beat up, it is no fun. No fun at all.

In fact, it soon became my least favorite thing in the world.

Now, before you go thinking I just had a bad attitude, let's be honest: Asian kids tend to be smaller than other kids their age. So Exhibit A in Why I Was Justified in Hating Judo: I was small. And even though we were all supposed to use our *skills* on the mat, the bigger kids used their strength instead (none of us had much in the way of skills at that age). So when I say I got beat up, I mean I got beat up. A lot.

Exhibit B? Well, because my older brother had already been doing judo for four years, he was obviously much better than I was.

He was almost always winning the tournaments we entered. And I was…not.

And I wasn't the only person who noticed my lack-of-winning streak either.

Cut to: me at a tournament relatively early in my judo days, but not so early that I hadn't already been to a good number of tournaments, standing on the sidelines, getting ready to go up against my opponent. As you might imagine, this was kind of a nerve-wracking moment for me. I was trying to remember tips my Sensei had given me and telling myself it wasn't like winning was everything, even though I knew it was. The announcer called out my opponent's name, and I froze. Then he called my name.

Before I could get my feet to move, I heard, "Oh, this is the younger Higa." It was coming from the man behind me.

I turned my head toward the voice slightly, almost as a reflex at hearing my last name.

"Not the good one," he said.

Ouch. I felt my face go hot. But I didn't react. I couldn't.

All I wanted to do in that moment was walk out of that tournament, go home, and forget about this whole judo thing. But of course I couldn't. I had to go out there in front of everyone, knowing they thought I wasn't any good. And prove them right, by not being as good as my brother, even though I was trying as hard as I could. (Well, actually I wasn't, but they didn't know that. They just thought I was bad. Which was how I felt.)

● ● ●

Okay, so let's leave little five-year-old Ryan right there, suffering away on the judo mat, getting his ass kicked, and go and meet up with him, also at age five, over on the basketball court. Now, as you'll remember, this was the age when my parents required me to do not only a martial art but also a team sport. For which I chose basketball.

Here's how well that went for me.

● ● ●

SCENE 1: AT PRACTICE[12]
COACH YELLING AT A BUNCH OF KIDS. KIDS RUNNING
AROUND IN A SAD ATTEMPT AT ORGANIZED PLAYS.
COACH YELLS SOME MORE.

[12] I know montages don't work as well in books as they do in movies, but it's my story and I'll montage if I want to.

Now, I'm no fan of getting yelled at, but in practice I could mostly blend in with the rest of the team and survive the group yelling-at until I was allowed to go home.

SCENE 2: OUR FIRST GAME

SOMEONE THROWS THE BALL TO RYAN. LOOK OF TERROR ON RYAN'S FACE. HE STARTS DRIBBLING AND...THE BALL IS STOLEN. COACH YELLS.

SCENE 3: SECOND GAME OF THE SEASON

PLAYERS RUNNING THE COURT IN AN ORDERLY-ISH FASHION. SOMEONE THROWS THE BALL TO YOUNG RYAN. HE FREEZES. COACH YELLS.

Some of my teammates had started to not suck. They'd picked up some moves from all the practice we'd had and looked like a real team.

But not me.

When the ball was thrown to me, it felt so much bigger and more awkward in my hands than I'd expected. I willed myself to dribble, but after my game-one experience it wasn't easy. The ball nearly got away from me, and I hadn't even started running yet.

In my mind, I knew what it was to dribble well, because I'd seen it done by my teammates. But *I* couldn't dribble well. And if I couldn't do it well, I didn't even want to try. So I didn't. Instead, I chose to pass the ball to one of my teammates as fast as I could before I really messed it up. If we had been playing Hot Potato, I would have ruled. Only I wasn't very coordinated. I threw it out-of-bounds. (So, no Hot Potato championship for Young Ryan either.)

SCENE 4: SOME OTHER GAME, WHO KNOWS WHICH ONE
RYAN FALLS DOWN, KNEES DRAGGING ALONG THE
POLISHED WOOD FLOOR WITH THIS HIDEOUS SQUEAKY
SHRIEK. COACH YELLS.

Ouch.

Yeah, basketball sucked. No, I sucked.

And I couldn't understand why this was happening. Like, why do I have to do something I'm not good at? Not being good when I was trying made me want to do even worse, to be a rebel, and to show everyone I didn't care. Not trying is like a safety net to prepare yourself for failure: If you don't care, being bad doesn't matter.

So I preferred not to try at all. It's like the opposite of that saying "Fake it until you make it." Something like, "If you know you can't make it, don't even bother to fake it." Hmm, I wonder why that never caught on as an inspirational catchphrase? It's got a definite ring to it.

IF YOU KNOW YOU CAN'T MAKE IT, DON'T EVEN BOTHER TO FAKE IT.

This was just how I was by nature. In school, I felt the same way. When my teacher tried to instruct me on how to write the letters of the alphabet, I crossed my arms and refused. I didn't want to do it ugly like a five-year-old. So I resisted doing it at all for as long as I could get away with doing nothing. I guess even as a five-year-old, I had some serious perfectionist tendencies—if I couldn't do it perfectly, then I was out.

WAY TO INSPIRE, RYAN.

I KNOW, I KNOW.

LOOKING BACK, THIS LOOKED LIKE IT WAS JUST ME BEING STUBBORN.

BUT I DIDN'T LIKE TO BE BAD AT THINGS.

I LIKED TO SEE PROGRESSION. WHEN I PUT MY TIME INTO SOMETHING,

I WANTED TO SEE MYSELF GETTING BETTER.

EVEN IF IT WAS BUILDING A FORT

OR PLAYING VIDEO GAMES.

Score
200

HP

I DIDN'T MIND PUTTING IN THE WORK, AS LONG AS I KNEW THAT I WAS GOING TO GET A RESULT.

AND WHEN I DIDN'T...

I'D JUST SIT BACK

AND DO NOTHING.

I WAS **GREAT** AT DOING NOTHING.

YOUR PARENTS MUST HAVE BEEN SO PROUD.

DANG,

YOU'RE REALLY GETTING THE HANG OF SARCASM.

OKAY, DID WE GIVE ENOUGH BACKSTORY?

WILL READERS GET THAT I WAS PRETTY MISERABLE FOR A LOT OF LITTLE REASONS THAT FELT LIKE THEY JUST KEPT PILING UP?

AND THAT I HATED WHEN I COULDN'T CONTROL AN OUTCOME?

YES.

BUT PROBABLY WHAT THEY'LL REMEMBER MOST IS THE PART WHERE YOUR TEACHER DESCRIBED YOU...

...AS AN OLD MAN IN A KID'S BODY.

SHE DESERVES A TEACHER OF THE YEAR AWARD FOR THAT.

...

SORRY.

WE CAN MOVE ON NOW.

A little backstory goes a long way. One of the most important elements of writing a book is keeping the main story moving. This lesson has to do with pacing, which is probably the place where things most often go wrong. We've all read books or seen movies where the action is about as exciting as a bowl of quinoa.[13] It seems like nothing is really happening and the story is going nowhere. Or we've tried to follow stories where there's so much action, it's impossible to tell what's happening, or why, or what it all means. That right there is some bad pacing, my friend. Ideally, a book should let readers figure out some elements of the story for themselves, while giving them enough information to do so. If I told you every detail of my life, you would be bored to tears, I promise. That's why we're going to jump ahead a little in time right now. And not just to where we left off the story back in Lesson 4, with my first day of sixth grade and the placement test and all that, but a few weeks later, after I'd settled into my regular middle-school routine.

[13] I just wanted to put the word *quinoa* somewhere in my book. So, check!

● ● ●

So a few weeks at my new school didn't exactly win me over to its merits or charms. Coming from a normal elementary school, I couldn't get over the fact that this charter "school" was like one-twentieth the size of my old school. I put that word in quotations because if anyone else saw what it looked like, *school* might not be the first word that came to mind.

The building was two stories and basically looked like a mini-mall. All the middle-school classes took place on the second floor. Naturally, there was only one staircase to get upstairs, and it looked like you could for sure get murdered while using it. Picture an enclosed staircase, one that Sarah Connor in *Terminator 2* might have run down while trying to escape from an insane asylum. It was all white with fluorescent lights and exposed pipes, and I always felt as if at any moment a half-decomposed, twitching dead woman might come crawling along like in *The Grudge*. Yes, I was terrified of that staircase. I don't ever recall walking up or down those stairs. I always ran.

● ● ●

If I was a metaphor guy, I'd say that those stairs were a metaphor for my entire experience at that school—except that they weren't a metaphor, they were real....

Also real: that test I took. Don't you want to know how I did?

● ● ●

I did well on the test. A little too well. I got moved into the group for the older kids. All the people I kind of knew and actually could have been friends with? Like Ardie? I didn't have any face time with them during the day. I didn't get to spend enough time with them to maintain a connection. So we weren't friends. After a while, we didn't even say hi anymore.

So here I was, the normal age you are when you start sixth grade, eleven years old. And I was in a class with all these kids who were the normal age you are when you start seventh grade: twelve years old. Plus, there were a few kids who'd been held back a year, and they were thirteen or fourteen.

Remember Mr. Boy Band? He was in my class.

But that's okay. No big deal.

This is great, I thought early on. *They're going to think I'm cool because I skipped a grade.*

●   ●   ●

Hahahahahahahahahahahahahahahahahahahahahahahahahahahahahaha hahahahahahahahahahahahahahahahahahahahahahahahahahahahahahaha hahahahahahahahahahahahahahahahahahahahahahahahahahahahahahaha hahahahahahahahahahahahahahahahahahahahahahahahahahahahahahaha hahahahahahahahahahahahahahahahahahahahahahahahahahahahahahaha hahahahahahahahahahahahahahahahahahahahahahahahahahahahahahaha…

Oh, man. Poor Young Ryan. It's hard to believe I was ever that naive and optimistic. But there it is, in black and white and italics.

●   ●   ●

It didn't take long for me to have a major reality check: *They think I'm the opposite of cool.*

Not only was I the youngest kid in my class, but I was also the smallest and one of only a few Asians. I was basically a (tiny) target.

One day not long into the school year, I was walking down the hall when I saw Mr. Boy Band. Let's call this kid Dick, because that's what he was.[14] Anyway, you know how it is between classes: All the students are rushing around, trying to run and grab that book they need before getting themselves to class on time. And everyone is talking. Or doing something stupid to catch the eye of the girl they like. Or the boy they like. Actually, no, it's mostly just the guys who act dumb, thinking it's somehow going to impress the girls. The point is, it was really loud and crowded.

And there was stupid Dick, with his stupid hair and his stupid surf shorts and T-shirt—typical local attire—standing there with his stupid friends, in the middle of everything, hulking over everyone, blocking out the sun. Okay, maybe he wasn't really *that* tall, but he was like six foot, which was pretty big for a middle schooler. To me, he might as well have been Godzilla. I walked by him, not knowing enough to get out of his way, as I soon would whenever I saw him. And without any good reason, he stuck out his leg and caught me at the ankles. I wasn't expecting it, so I stumbled a few feet, and I couldn't catch my balance. I flailed my arms around, trying to right myself.

But there was no avoiding it.

I was going down.

I fell forward onto the floor. And remember all those people jostling one another and rushing around me? They stopped to watch.

---

[14] If you've seen my *Draw My Life* video, this part will be familiar to you. Feel free to skip ahead if you want, but because this is a book, I do go into a little more detail here. Just saying.

Dick started laughing. Then his stupid friends started laughing. Some of the kids who'd stopped to see what was happening laughed too. Not because they'd seen a bully trip the little Asian kid. (Only Dick and his friends knew what had really happened.) But because they'd seen the little Asian kid rushing to class (which I was, to avoid the awkwardness of not having any friends to walk with me). And they'd assumed that my speed walk had tripped me up and brought me down.

Which was way more embarrassing, actually. And it didn't do anything for my image (or my self-image).

I felt all my blood rush to my face as I burned with humiliation. I scrambled up as quickly as I could, kept my head down, and went straight to my next class. The rest of the day, I tried to ignore Dick. When I saw him in the hallway, I ducked behind another kid, trying to melt into the crowd, but I could feel him watching me, laughing at me with his friends. He'd gotten to me, and he knew it.

That afternoon when my mom picked me up, she had the smile on her face she always had. "How was school?" she asked, like she did every day.

I had been playing along for the most part (which meant a muttered "fine" and a half scowl in response to her relentless enthusiasm). But no more. The memory of everyone laughing at me while I was splayed out on the ground had been on a constant loop in my brain all day. I couldn't play along anymore. "Why do I have to go to this school?" I said.

"We've talked about this, Ryan. This school is better than that other school," she said.

I didn't even know how to respond to her. It was the same thing she'd been telling me all along. All I could do was sit there and think, *It doesn't feel better. It feels awful.* And try very hard not to cry.

I kept quiet the rest of the ride to basketball practice. Normally I would have been making jokes, talking about something or other. But not today. There was nothing to say. My mom looked over at me, but I turned away and watched the view out the window.

And that's how my life was for a while—that day on repeat. Get picked on at school. Get picked up by my mom. Go to basketball. Get yelled at by the coach. Go to judo. Get yelled at by the Sensei. Go home and do tons of homework. Go to bed and toss and turn, unable to sleep. And then get out of bed at dawn and do the whole thing again.

At first, when I was at home, I was fine. I was able to shake it off and do my usual thing—joking around, hanging out with my friends in the neighborhood. My dad had no idea how much I hated middle school. But the minute Mom and I got into the car to drive to school in the morning, I'd feel this dread creeping over me. Soon I started keeping to myself, unable to hide how unhappy I was.

One morning, not long after my "trip" in the hallway, I came up with a plan. The greatest plan ever. Surely, I was the first person to think of this! When I walked out of my bedroom in the morning, I moved slowly, like that was as fast as I could go. I found my mom in the kitchen, ready to drive me to school.

"I feel sick," I said.

"You don't look sick," she said.

"I have a headache."

She just gave me a look.

She put her hand on my forehead. I realized then that no amount of sad puppy-dog eyes would heat up my forehead enough to feel like I had a fever. "You're fine," she said. "We have to leave or we'll be late."

If only my mom had known how wrong she was. I may not have been sick that morning, but I was far from fine.

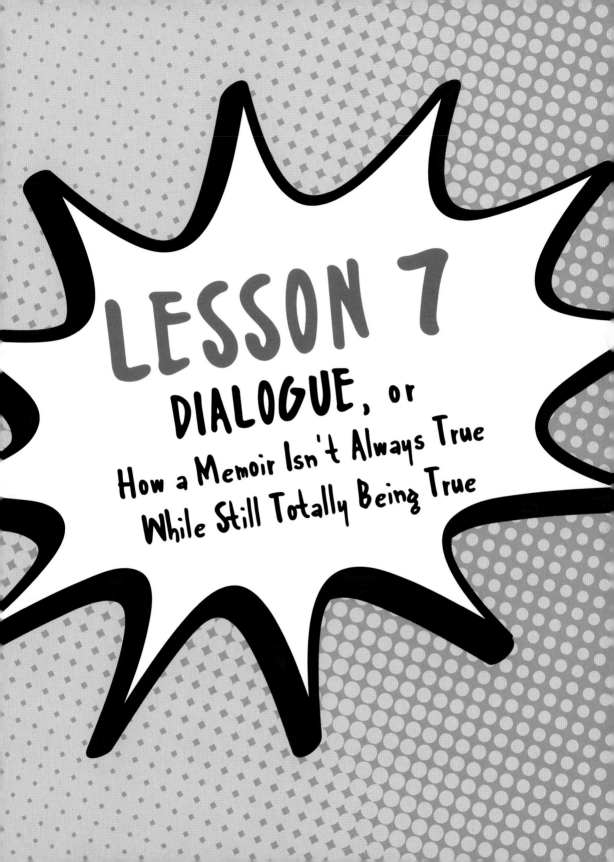

LESSON 7

DIALOGUE, or

How a Memoir Isn't Always True
While Still Totally Being True

WHAT KIND OF
CHAPTER TITLE
IS THAT?

YOU'VE GOT A
BETTER ONE?

I THOUGHT YOU
WERE SUPPOSED TO
HAVE A WAY WITH
WORDS.

IT'S CALLED
HUMOR.

There are two main kinds of books: fiction and nonfiction. Fiction books are totally made up. They may resemble real life in some ways. But the writer invented every single word. Or even if the writer drew some of the characters and events from their own life or history, they didn't feel any necessity to stick to the facts. They exaggerated whenever they wanted to, in order to tell the kind of story they were trying to share with their readers. Now, a nonfiction book, such as a memoir like this one, is true. That means that everything in it happened and is being recounted as clearly as the author can remember it. But here's the thing: Memory is tricky. Especially because, when we're living our lives, most of us aren't thinking: *Oh, oh, oh, I'd better remember this exactly as it happened so I can write it all down and turn it into a book someday.* But nonfiction writers have an obligation to their readers to try to be as accurate as possible, while also making the story, y'know, a story. See, there is no way the dialogue in any memoir happened exactly the way it appears in the book. So writers fill in the blanks of their memory. Like I'm about to do....

• • •

Just my luck, Dick had a posse, all older than me, all stupid jerks. This horrible guy, let's call him Brad. And two terrible girls, Jasmine and Cassidy, who were scary and big, not like overweight, just like *big*. Jasmine wore a lot of bright colors and sparkles. It filled me with dread just to see her coming down the hall toward me, glinting and glittering in the light (gloom and doom come in all styles). And Cassidy was smaller and skinny, but still bigger than me (it didn't take much back then), and she was very sassy. She was the kind of girl who thought she was all that. I avoided all these kids at all costs. Sometimes when I saw them I even turned and walked the other way, or ducked into the bathroom. But when Dick tripped me, they'd gotten their first taste of blood, and they were hungry for more.

Insults. Shoves. Cruel laughter.

That was my life at school now. Every day.

LOOKING BACK, I CAN SEE THAT DICK AND HIS CREW WERE JERKS TO BASICALLY EVERYONE IN OUR CLASS. BUT THAT DIDN'T MAKE ME FEEL ANY BETTER, BECAUSE THEY SO OBVIOUSLY SINGLED ME OUT.

BEING THE YOUNGEST AND SMALLEST WAS BASICALLY LIKE BEING THE WEAKEST ANTELOPE IN THE HERD.

HIGH-FIVE!

WHAT, FOR BEING THE WEAKEST ANTELOPE?

AND YOU CALLED **ME** DARK?

NO, NO SORRY. I WAS GIVING YOU PROPS FOR THAT RAD SIMILE.

OH YEAH, SURE, HIGH-FIVE.

I've always had an analytical mind, so I'd lie awake at night, unable to fall asleep, thinking about what was happening to me at school and trying to figure out how I could make it stop. I decided to work my way through all my possible options. I was going to find a solution and then convince my mom, no matter what.

I had already asked my mom why I had to go to Charter World Charter School.[15] Her answer was always some form of:

"Because it's the best education for you."

So I knew going into this that I had to improve on the Tri-Beam Offensive and be more targeted in my approach. Soon enough, I figured out that I had to go down the

---

[15] I mean, I might have asked her more than once....

specific logic paths that I knew my mom would relate to and say things that I knew would appeal to her. I analyzed her thought process, so I could outsmart her: *Okay, she wants me to go here for the education. So I'm going to tell her I'm not learning anything.*

Because…

I can't hear my teachers.

Because…

This building wasn't even meant to be a school, and the walls are basically made of portable chalkboards and don't even go all the way up to the ceiling![16] So I hear the class next door instead of my own teacher in my classroom.

Ryan tries to convince Mom to let him change schools:

INTERIOR CAR, AT SCHOOL PICKUP:

Take 1!

"I don't see why I have to go here," I say. "This school isn't teaching me anything. I can't even hear my teacher half the time. I only hear the class next door."

"You're getting good grades, and you seem to be doing well," she says.

That's hard to argue with, so again, end of discussion.

Take 2!

"My math teacher is so smart he's weird. He's teaching us stuff that's not even in the book."

"Wow, he's challenging you guys to think outside the box. That's great."

Take 3!

"They don't give us enough lunch. I'm still hungry."

"We have time. Let's pick up something to eat before your practice."

---

[16] This is true. Seriously, how did they expect kids to learn in that environment?

No matter what approach I tried, my mom wouldn't budge and my dad wasn't much help either.

Take 4!

"Hey, Dad, I was wondering if—"

"Talk to your mom…"

I didn't realize it at the time, but I was trying to figure out a why for everything. It was just a natural question in my head. And the biggest *why* of all?

Why is this happening to me?

When I'd started at this new school a few weeks earlier, I'd hoped to fit in and make friends. Not like I had to be the most popular kid in my class, but I'd always had a crew. People liked me. And I was used to staying out of trouble and being one of the best students in my class. Soon I didn't care about any of that anymore. My biggest hope every day was to not get noticed. I started to pretend that I wasn't smart and I didn't know the answers in class.

But that didn't help.

Outside of class, I did my best to disappear. I tried to avoid Dick and his friends in the hallway between classes by slipping behind other students when I found myself trapped in their line of sight.

But that didn't help.

Nothing helped.

One day, I went to a school assembly held at the bandstand in the park. Because the school was in a small building, there wasn't an area big enough to have all the students together. So whenever they wanted to get us all together for something, they had us walk across the street to the public park. By the time I arrived, there was nowhere to sit. And the last thing I wanted was to be the only kid in the entire school who was standing up. Standing up was standing out, and my basic survival routine did not permit that.

My one option was grim: The only open seat was right next to Jasmine and Cassidy. I looked at their glowering faces, sparkles blinding me in the sunlight. I wanted to turn around, walk out of that park, and never come back to school. But I had no choice. With the seconds ticking away, and my heart thunking in my chest, I squeezed myself onto the bleacher next to them, willing them to not notice me. But since I lack the power of mind control, I had no such luck.

"What do you think you're doing?" Cassidy asked in my general direction. (She never looked right at me.)

"Sitting," I stammered. "There's no place else to sit."

"Well, you can't sit here either, little ugly Chink boy," Jasmine said, laughing.

And then, laughing hideously, they pushed me off the bleacher. Everyone around us saw me fall and started laughing. My cheeks burned with humiliation. I was in a crowd of people, yet I felt so totally alone. I sprang up, trying to get away from them as quickly as I could. Even when I was far away from them and they were nowhere in sight, I couldn't stop replaying in my head what had happened.

They called me ugly. Fine. I was used to that. They shoved me and people laughed. Okay, yeah, I'd managed to avoid that level of public humiliation for a while, so I guess my streak was over. But they called me a Chink?! So. Not. Okay. It was racist and offensive on so many levels. I'm not even Chinese! My thoughts twisted with embarrassment and rage.

My life at school had been terrible for weeks, but that was the final straw.

When my mom came to pick me up that day, I was done trying to outsmart her or convince her. I just wanted the bullying to stop. I hadn't told anyone about it—not my family or my neighborhood friends—but now I couldn't keep it in.

Before my mom could even finish her usual "How was school today?" I blurted out, "These two stupid girls in my class who always make fun of me pushed me off the bleachers today." And then I told her what had happened.

"Oh, my goodness," my mom said. "Are you okay?"

"No!" I said. "I hate this school and I can't believe you're still making me go!"

"There are teachers at the other school who are unhappy and act like they don't want to be there. The teachers at this school have chosen to be here. It's really the best place to—"

HEY, TOMLINSON, YOU'RE SURE IT'S OKAY TO MAKE UP DIALOGUE FOR THIS SCENE?

WOULD I LIE TO YOU?

I HOPE NOT. BUT I DON'T WANT TO LIE TO MY READERS. I REALLY DON'T REMEMBER EXACTLY WHAT MY MOM AND I SAID THAT DAY. AND MY MOM DOESN'T REMEMBER EITHER.

SO I'M RE-CREATING THIS SCENE BASED ON WHAT I **DO** REMEMBER AND WHAT I KNOW TO BE TRUE ABOUT MYSELF AT THAT AGE.

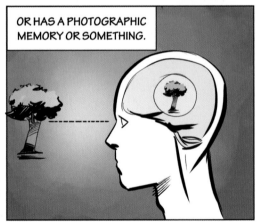

I hadn't wanted to tell my mom—or anyone—what was going down at school. But once I did, I felt a huge rush of relief. Finally, something was going to happen. Maybe…maybe, it'd even get better.

But of course it didn't. My mom called the principal the next day, and he said he would absolutely take care of it. I imagined Jasmine and Cassidy getting expelled, or at the very least suspended. But instead he called an assembly and gave an informal lecture to the whole school about bullying, or what he called "respecting our fellow students."

At first I was afraid that everyone would know the principal was talking about me. But no one seemed to be looking at me. So I started to sit up a little bit straighter. I even felt hopeful for the first time in that whole, long, awful school year. Finally, I thought I would catch a break and life would get at least a little better, easier.

But.

That very afternoon, Dick made good on his name and called me a "gay faggot."[17] And of course people laughed. And the by-now-familiar feeling of humiliation settled in.

When my mom picked me up from school that day, she asked hesitantly, "So how did it go today?"

"Bad, just like always," I said, looking out the window, not wanting to talk.

"Things will get better," she said.

It was a nice thought. But my analytical mind told me otherwise: *I broke down and told my mom, and she talked to the principal, and yet it definitely wasn't better at school today than it was yesterday. And now I'm out of options for trying to change any-thing. And it's certainly not going to get better tomorrow all by itself.*

I'd tried keeping to myself.

I'd tried figuring out a solution.

I'd tried asking for help.

I felt more powerless than ever. No one could help me.

So I'd have to help myself.

And with that, an old familiar caller returned, and not someone I'd exactly call a friend either. My thoughts about death came back, more persistent than ever. It seemed like my best option.

---

17 *Good ol' Dick sure had a way with words.*

DON'T WORRY...

...THERE'LL BE A NICE, SHINY LESSON FOR EVERYONE AT THE END OF IT ALL.

OOH, A LESSON.

CAN WE PUT A BOW ON IT?

...

NO BOW, OF COURSE. NO BOW.

THAT WAS A TERRIBLE IDEA. OKAY, LET THE DARKNESS CONTINUE.

I'M A GHOST. YOU CAN'T SCARE ME.

I WOULDN'T EVEN TRY.

BUT BEFORE WE DESCEND INTO DARKNESS...

I'M GONNA GRAB SOMETHING TO EAT.

REALLY?

WE'RE DOING THAT AGAIN?

YES, REALLY.

LESSON 8

IT'S ALL IN THE
DETAILS

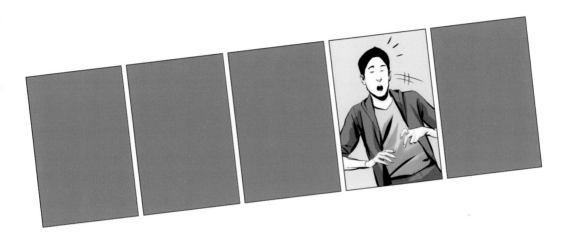

Did you know that a writer can reveal things about his character by deciding what telling details to include on the page? (I didn't know either, but it totally makes sense.) This doesn't mean writing down every descriptive item you remember, just because you can. As the storyteller, you're making a choice about what to show your reader, in order to create a full picture. Like, you could just describe your character's T-shirt as blue and old, but if you point out that the blue shirt is faded and the fabric is worn thin, you're *showing* that it's old instead of just telling the reader. Believe me, a book of just telling is no fun to read. I should know—that's how the first draft of this book was, and even I had a hard time keeping my eyes open when I was trying to rework it.

With details, you can also dig a little deeper for descriptive elements that will tell the reader who the hero *really* is. Like how short he was compared with other boys his age, because that's what made him a target for bullies. Or if he wore a *Dragon Ball Z* backpack to middle school every day. Because that was his favorite TV show and the source of his hope that, like its hero, he would eventually triumph too.

HEY! DID YOU JUST ADD THAT DETAIL WHILE I WAS GETTING A SNACK?

DRAGON BALL Z MAY HAVE BEEN MY FAVORITE SHOW...

...BUT EVEN I KNEW BETTER THAN TO WEAR A BACKPACK ADVERTISING THE FACT.

IT WASN'T COOL TO BE INTO NERDY THINGS BACK THEN.

AND...I THINK WE'VE HIT A VEIN.

THE FACT THAT THESE DETAILS BRING UP SO MUCH EMOTION FOR YOU SHOWS THAT THEY REALLY TELL THE READER SOMETHING IMPORTANT ABOUT YOUR MIDDLE-SCHOOL SELF!

SOMETIMES IT'S THE EMBARASSING SPECIFICS THAT ARE MOST REVEALING.

UGH.

I CAN SEE YOUR POINT.

THANK YOU!

BUT YOU CAN'T JUST ADD IN DETAILS WHEN I'M NOT LOOKING.

YOU GOT IT, BOSS.

So, now, getting back to the story. As you may remember, when you last saw Young Ryan, he was a few weeks into middle school. And hating it. Let's add some description.

True Facts about Young Ryan:

Didn't pay attention in class.

Didn't like getting in trouble for not paying attention in class.

Hated school.

Did well in school.

Wished other kids would be nicer to him.

Didn't go out of his way to make friends, because he was sure that everyone was mean.

The funny thing about this list is that, while these are all true facts, they're also pretty contradictory. That's probably the hardest thing about picking descriptions to include when you're writing a book. As soon as you make one statement about something, you might realize that the opposite statement is true too. Or partially true. And then it all gets kind of blurry. But how I remember it is how I've got to tell it.

● ● ●

There was basically only one bright point in my day. Ever since I was a young kid, I'd always watched a ton of movies and TV shows, and I even thought I wanted to be an actor when I grew up. Comedy was my favorite. Especially anything with Ben Stiller (*Zoolander* was, hands down, my favorite movie when I was a kid). Or Jim Carrey (I lost count of how many times I watched *Ace Ventura*, *Dumb & Dumber*, and *Liar Liar*). I liked action movies too, but action movies like *Kill Bill*—ones that were a little over the top. And tons of cartoon and anime, especially *Pokeman* and *Dragon Ball Z*. A little trivia: I collected all the *Dragon Ball Z* VHS tapes, and when you lined them up in order with the spines out, it created a really cool picture.

As much as I loved TV and movies, they only provided a temporary escape. No matter how many fictional worlds I lost myself in, they wouldn't improve my tortured existence in my real life.

Usually I was pretty good at using my logical approach to make things work out in my favor, but I'd tried every argument and technique I could think of to make my life better (or at least not as awful). And nothing had helped. At all.

All I knew was:

Nobody listened to me.

Nobody cared what I wanted.

I existed at school only to be a target.

At home, my brother often made me feel the same way.

The only real friends I had were neighborhood kids—the guys I should've been in school with—and my parents kept me so busy with all the things I had to do every day that I had no time to see them.

My treat after judo practice was McDonald's. But come on. A Happy Meal is not enough happiness to live on.[18]

By the time I got into bed every night, I was exhausted from a long day of feeling anxious and awful. But I couldn't sleep. Because I knew the next day would be more of the same: more frustration, more dread, more misery, more humiliation. I wanted the horror to end. At first, I'd lie awake in the darkness of my bedroom and obsessively analyze my situation in search of an out. When I didn't come up with a solution after a couple of months, my obsessive thoughts changed to fantasies.

Dark fantasies.

Angry fantasies.

Some days, my brother messed with me after school when I was already deeply unhappy.

Like, I'd be waiting for my turn on the computer and he would basically just ignore me.

"I'm still playing my game," was his usual reply. And then he'd push me, like I was a fly he could swat away. Since he was older and bigger (and, of course, better at judo), I knew better than to push back.

I'd replay the scene in my mind. Only this time, instead of him getting the upper hand, as he always did, I had a new vision: *I punched him in the head. He clutched his face, groaning in pain, and fell back, finally leaving me in peace.*

It was the same thing with the jerks from school.

If Dick had pushed me or called me ugly at school that day (and if it was a day that I was at school, you can assume he had), I edited the scene in my mind so that

[18] Unless of course McDonald's wants to become the official sponsor of this book, then of course it is!

this time, I took my ruler and stabbed him in the eye. He started screaming, and there was blood everywhere…and it felt great.

I didn't even want to fit in anymore. After the humiliation I'd suffered at the recent school assembly, plus the fact that I had finally told someone and *still* nothing changed—I was way beyond the point of wanting things to be normal. By now, I had mean urges. Evil thoughts.

Because I took judo, I knew I could defend myself, even though I was small. My fantasies grew more involved. And more violent. But still, because I was always highly analytical, there was an inevitable logic even to my fantasies:

One day I'm just going to snap and fight them.

But I don't want to deal with the consequences of getting in trouble.

So I'll just kill myself.

Day after bad day, night after sleepless night, it really started to feel like the best option. I became obsessed with the thought of dying.

Where do you go when you die?

Is it like falling asleep?

I wouldn't have to deal with any of this if I wasn't alive. If it's just like going to sleep, and then it's like, well…nothing. That might not be too bad.

Now I just had to figure out a way to do it.

My first idea was to overdose on sleeping pills. But my mind was logical about this too. I went online and looked at suicide forums, and the general consensus was that this approach was painful and usually didn't work.[19] While I had managed to deal with emotional pain, inflicting physical pain on myself was not something I could commit to at that point. And where did I think I was going to get a bunch of sleeping pills anyhow? So that was out.

---

[19] It was like Yelp for suicide methods. "If I could give pills less than one star, I would. Hurt like hell and then didn't even work!"

I thought I could slit my wrists. But that would hurt too. So that was out.

I thought I could jump off a building. But I was afraid of heights. So that was out too.

I wasn't sure *how* I'd do it. But I knew I'd do it if I had to.

The thought of dying didn't scare me—it was the getting-dead part I was having a problem with. Imagining being dead felt good, like a form of power during days of complete and total powerlessness and misery.

But those were just fantasies I had when I couldn't sleep at night. I never talked about them to anyone. During the day, I still had to suffer through the long hours of school. I had started to feel like a different person. From the moment I got out of my mom's car in the morning and walked up to that sham of a school building, it was like I was expending all my energy on trying to create a force field—I just wanted to be invisible.

One day, after Dick did that leg-tripping game that was popular at the time—where you walk behind someone and then sweep their back leg so it would get stuck behind their other leg, causing them to miss their next step—I couldn't take it any-more. Once he got a laugh, he kept walking, sailing down the hallway like he didn't have a care in the world. Meanwhile, there I was, all the anger and humiliation and hopelessness I'd been feeling every day for months bubbling up. It's like it was too big to stay inside me. Before I even knew what I was doing, I ran into one of the empty classrooms, my ears ringing with anger, my face flushed with embarrassment.

Stupid jerk. My mind raced with rage. I couldn't control it. *BAM*, I hit the wall. Literally.

I looked at my hand, my knuckles red from the impact. The pain felt good. At least it was real.

At least it was fair.

WOW.

I'M SORRY YOU HAD TO GO THROUGH THAT.

IT HAPPENS. ONE OF THE MAIN REASONS I WANTED TO WRITE THIS BOOK WAS TO TALK ABOUT MY BULLYING. AFTER I POSTED MY **DRAW MY LIFE** VIDEO, I HEARD FROM SO MANY PEOPLE WHO'D GONE THROUGH SOMETHING SIMILAR.

KIDS ARE THE WORST.

SOME OF THEM ARE, SURE.

BUT ALL THE FEEDBACK REALLY MADE AN IMPACT ON ME. BECAUSE I KNOW HOW CLOSE I CAME TO KILLING MYSELF.

AND I HATE TO THINK OF ANY OF MY READERS GOING TO A PLACE THAT DARK.

IF I COULD TELL YOUNG RYAN ONE THING, IT'D BE...

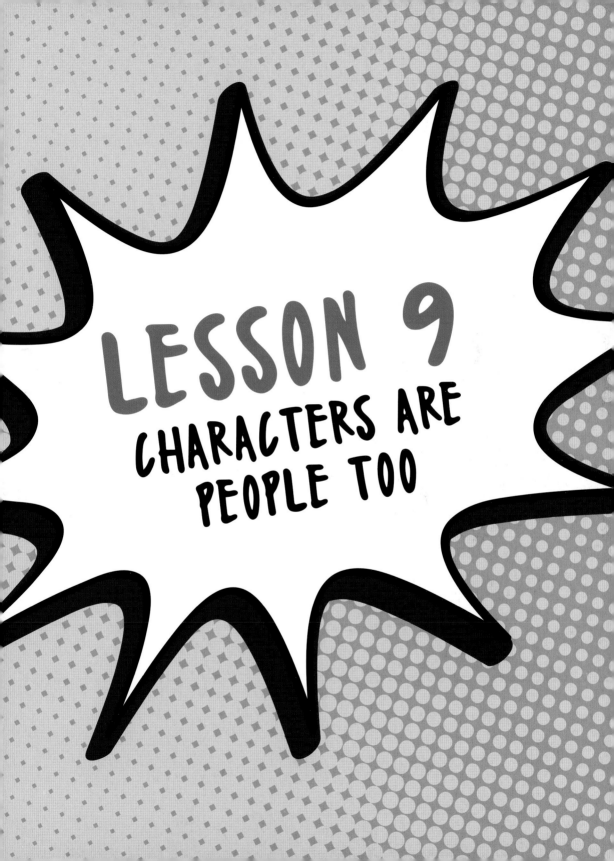

Okay, listen up so this doesn't get confusing. In our last lesson, I know we just talked about using details to better understand a character. Which may sound like character development, which is what this chapter is about. But not quite. Character development is how the character develops, not how the writer develops the character.[20] So it's how a character takes all his or her unique qualities (the ones we included in our description) and makes a choice, or takes an action, or responds to circumstances in some way. It's usually not an easy path to take (because that would be pretty boring, right?), but he does it anyhow. Or it doesn't go well at first, but he keeps trying. Basically, even though it feels like life is telling him to stay in bed, pull the covers over his head, and give up, he's not going to do that. He's going to dig deep, grow in some way, and move the story forward with the kind of personal progress that's worth writing about. And that, right there, is character development.

[20] That might sound like some serious chicken-and-egg stuff right there, but you get what I'm saying, right? If not, I'm sure I'll hear about it in the comments below. OH WAIT, there are no comments below in a book. La la la la I really can't hear you....

●   ●   ●

One by one, the days passed in general misery, and the end of the school year arrived. When I walked out of the building that last day, I kept my head down as usual to avoid making eye contact with anyone and inadvertently inviting ridicule, but I felt a lightness I hadn't felt in months. I walked with purpose toward my mom's car and didn't turn back once. I had survived my first year of middle school.

When I woke up on the first morning of summer vacation, I was...relieved? Happy? I don't know exactly what I was feeling, but I know what I was thinking:

No Dick.

No Jasmine and Cassidy.

No Brad.

No class.

No homework.

No lying awake at night, worrying.

Well, maybe not so much that last one. It was hard to forget that there was a new year of middle school looming just a few months away. Plus judo and basketball were both year-round. I mean, I was still me, after all, excessive worrier and analyzer of all things analyzable (so: all things).

But away from the daily torment, I got a little perspective. My days were filled with playing video games and hanging out with my friends—people who actually liked me and didn't think of me only as the butt of their jokes. While I still fantasized about hurting my bullies, now that I was away from their daily abuse, the fantasies weren't on a constant loop in my brain. I didn't feel so dark inside. While we were playing hoops once and someone tripped me by accident, I thought about talking to my friends about what had been happening at school, but they all seemed to have had a fine school year, and even thinking about telling them made me feel alone and humiliated all over again. So I kept it to myself. They didn't need to hear about my sad existence. It started to seem like someone else's life.

One midsummer morning, I was sitting at the table eating breakfast and realized it had been a few days since I'd even thought about Dick and his crew.

"What are you smiling about?" Kyle asked.

"Nothing." I hadn't even realized I had been smiling.

He walked away, giving me a WTF look.

But as I lay awake in bed that night, my thoughts wandered to what I had been thinking about when my brother called me out for smiling. And it was this: I realized that my desire to kill myself had really been a desire to be able to hurt people back without punishment. It was a desire for the abuse to end. And thanks to summer vacation, it had. I knew there was a better than good chance that it would start up again when school did, but I also knew, deep down, that I didn't want to die. I had survived the year of regular torment; I wasn't going to kill myself now.

Maybe now I was a little less tortured, a little less miserable and trapped, a little less at the end of my rope. And that felt good, at least by comparison. But I still had to find a way to make my life better, if I was going to survive seventh grade. Nothing immediately sprang to mind.

Rather than think about ways to die, I now focused on ways to live. After all, if I'd been desperate enough to seriously consider killing myself, then clearly I'd reached a *What have I got to lose?* phase of my life.

I might as well try to make my situation better.

How could it be any worse?

From there, I played on that thought, and I started to ask myself why everything had happened like it had during my sixth-grade year. Here I was, back to *Why?*

Why me?

Why is life so unfair?

Why did Dick pick on me in the first place?

That's when I figured it out: *He did it to make people laugh. It was comedy.*

I reasoned that the bullies wouldn't just leave me alone, because their antics earned them laughs from their classmates, and it was the laughs that made them popular. That's what everyone seemed to want in this world: a laugh. Popularity.

A new thought took hold.

It was the one thought that gave me hope: *Go for the funny.*

Laughs seemed to be what drove the bullies. I mean, sure, Dick and the others seemed to genuinely enjoy humiliating me, but they never did it in private—only when people could see…and laugh. This could be the key to everything for me too.

In place of my fantasies about hurting myself, or others, I started having a new thought: *If I want to beat my bullies, I need to take the funny away from them.*

So I started analyzing the bullies' behavior and my classmates' reactions.

Why had they laughed the moment I got pushed down?

Why had they responded the way they did?

Why do people even laugh in the first place?

Again and again, it always seemed to come down to that one question: *Why?*

By the time school started again, I was actually feeling better about where I was at in life. It helped that Dick and Cassidy had left school and weren't around to bother me anymore.

But I still had Jasmine and Brad in my class, and even though there were a couple of new kids this year, I was still the biggest (i.e., smallest) target in sight (no growth spurt *yet*).

And then, in English class, we got the absolute worst assignment of all time.

We had to memorize a poem and recite it in class. I was already deathly afraid of public speaking under the best of circumstances (if such a thing even exists). And being in a classroom full of people who were always looking out for ways to humiliate me, well, that was pretty much the *worst* of circumstances. I knew, no matter how it went for me, I was going to be made fun of for what I said, or how I said it, or whatever "it" was the bullies singled out in me. There was no winning.

This was the perfect storm of circumstances to really set off Brad and Jasmine. I'd be standing up in front of the class, all by myself, with nowhere to hide. One misstep, and they'd use it as ammunition to tease me mercilessly. Forever.

I needed a plan.

The night before my presentation, I pictured myself frozen at the front of the room, all eyes on me, my stomach queasy with nerves, my mouth dry with dread.

Then it hit me. More than a plan, I needed a comeback.

Why, can you do it better yourself? I heard in my head.

That's it! If my bullies say anything mean, I know what to say to shut them up.

From there, it was as if the floodgates of good ideas opened up. I thought about all the comebacks I could make, reacting to anything mean they might say.

Meanwhile, I kept practicing the poem[21] I had to recite, hoping I wouldn't mess up. But I already felt less scared. Even if the worst happened, I knew what to say. And I also knew how I had to feel in order to survive, no matter what:

Just don't care. Don't care about anything. And you'll be fine.

I was about as prepared as it was possible to be.

---

[21] My editor really wanted to know which poem it was—"details are important," she told me—but the only details I can clearly recall involve trying to make it out of this assignment alive.

I was even prepared for what to do when my preparations failed.

Still, I was basically expecting it all to go awfully.

I mean, that's pretty much how every day of the previous year had gone, right? And I had survived, so I could survive this too. No matter what happened. Besides, I figured: *Preparing for the worst is better than hoping for the best and being disappointed.*

I was nervous all day. The minutes kept slipping away. And then, finally, there was no avoiding it anymore. There I was, standing in front of my classmates.

Catching sight of Brad, I pulled my eyes away immediately (never risk eye contact with the Beast). On the other side of the room, the light glared off Jasmine's sparkles. Again, I avoided her eyes. I could feel the sneering glares from her and Brad, without needing to see them. It's not like any of them had done well on their poems. But that just made me more nervous, more certain they'd want to put the focus on me. And my failure.

I opened my mouth.

I knew the first word of the poem, and the word after that. I recited it pretty much perfectly. But I don't think I would have been able to choke out even one word if I hadn't had those backup responses ready in my head.

Even more important than the fact that the poem went well, I'd finally found an out: If I could think up the perfect comeback—even if I never said it—it made life so much better, and I didn't feel so powerless all the time.

As seventh grade progressed, life actually wasn't so bad. I finally had a few friends, or at least people to say hello to in school. But it's not like the bullying stopped, which still sucked.

And so my analysis continued.

Since what made the bullies and their audience laugh hardest was when I became visibly upset by something they did to me, I realized that I had to hide my reaction. Then I'd steal their laugh. And there wouldn't be any reason to pick on me.

The next day, I went to school, and Brad caught me as I walked out of our classroom.

"Hey, ugly," he said.

This is when I finally stood up to him and said, "This ends today. You have wasted too much of my time and energy with your stupid, groundless insults. It's clear that your attempts to belittle me stem from your own deep insecurities and your pathetic need to be liked by our classmates. Well, I've had enough. Going forward, your words have no power over me. In fact, I can no longer even hear you. So don't bother speaking to me."

●　　●　　●

Okay, yeah, that didn't happen. It was more like this:

Instead of admitting that his words hurt my feelings, by frowning, or stopping to look around and see if anyone else had heard him and was reacting, I just kept on walking, as if he hadn't said anything at all. As I moved away, I could hear a few people laughing. But now that I wasn't standing there, frozen, showing everyone just how upset I was, it wasn't the same uproar the bully usually earned.

My plan had worked. A little, at least.

The next day, I vowed to take my counterattack one step further:

By going for a laugh of my own.

I saw Brad in the hallway, and instead of ducking behind a taller kid or trying to avoid him, I walked right toward him.

"Hey, ugly," he said.

This time, I stopped right in front of him. A few people started to laugh.

But instead of letting on that I was hurt, or upset,[22] I made a purposely ugly

---

[22] TBH, at this point, it's not like being called "ugly" hurt me anymore. I was used to it. It was more the endlessness of the attacks, if that makes sense?

face, with my eyes crossed and my nose scrunched up and my tongue hanging out.

"What? Me?" I said.

I actually got a BIGGER laugh than Brad had gotten. And no surprise either. Remember how I was always a big Jim Carrey fan? His comedy is essentially an encyclopedia of awesome facial expressions, and I'd studied them all.

I could hardly keep from smiling as I walked away down the hall, actually feeling good at school for the first time since I'd started at this hellhole the previous year. This was a GROUNDBREAKING MOMENT of realization that "going for the funny" actually worked!

From then on, I had it down. I'd beat my bullies to their insults by making fun of myself first, stealing their laughs from them altogether. I turned my analysis to what makes people laugh the hardest, and I tweaked my jokes accordingly, like a comedian working on his material, until I was getting laughs of my own. Or kind of like that last rap battle that Eminem did in *8 Mile*, except that the movie didn't exist at the time, so he pretty much stole my idea. It's all good, though. Me and Eminem are like BFFs now.[23]

---

[23] **Not really.**

It never hurts to add a romantic plotline.

• • •

School was still lame, but it wasn't the most terrible, awful place in the world anymore.

And then something happened that made my life even a little bit better. A piece of technology that was earth-shattering, mind-bending, life-changing! My older brother and my basketball teammates started getting into…MSN Messenger.[24]

One day, I came into the den, where Kyle was on the family computer.

"What are you doing?" I asked.

"Just talking to some friends on MSN Messenger."

"Will you set up an account for me?" I asked.

"Why? You don't have any friends," my brother said.

"That doesn't stop you, loser," I said.

(Aw, the international language of siblings.)

Anyhow, he set up an account for me. And when he finally got off the computer after hogging it all night, even though we were supposed to both get an equal amount of computer time, I knew exactly what I was going to do.

In the past year and a half, I had never stopped thinking about Nicole. She was the perfect girl for me. I just knew she was, even though she'd never noticed me, *and* we went to different schools now. She was beautiful. She was flawless. Like all the great romances throughout the ages, our love was eternal and predestined.

We were meant to be together. And soon our hearts would beat as one.

---

[24] For all you young'uns, this is basically like Facebook Messenger before Facebook even existed.

I got her MSN name and sent her an invitation to message.

She accepted.

It was as if we spoke a language that only we two could understand.

I wrote her a poem, twenty-one verses in all, comparing her to a sunset, a rainbow, a unicorn. I invited her out on a romantic hot-air balloon ride, complete with a violin player and a picnic featuring all her favorite foods. I knew her answer, even before she accepted, because already we were joined.

Actually.

It went more like this. When she said yes to my invitation, I thought: *OMG. She accepted! What should I say?*

I busted my brains thinking of something witty or cool.

How are you? I wrote.

I could barely sit still as I watched the cursor flashing on the screen, signaling that she was writing her response at this very moment.

Fine, she wrote back.

No way! Nicole and I are actually talking…or at least typing.

Finally, gathering all my courage, I sent her a message that read:

Will you go out with me?

My stomach a mess of knots, I sat and watched the blinking cursor, waiting for her reply. When it arrived, it was just one word:

No.

I sat there, stunned, waiting for more, an explanation, an excuse.

None arrived.[25]

There it was again: that familiar feeling that I was nothing, and nothing I wanted or cared about would ever go my way. There was no comeback for that.

Luckily, I was about to discover a passion of a different sort. One that couldn't reject me.

---

[25] Okay, it didn't happen that quickly. We had actually been chatting all summer but I'm skipping all the irrelevant small talk.

THAT'S A GREAT START. NOW GIVE US THE HAPPY ENDING WITH NICOLE.

...

THERE'S NO HAPPY ENDING?

...

OHHHH... SORRY...

I TOLD YOU THAT YOU SHOULD WAIT TO SEE HOW IT WENT.

LESSON II

VOICE[26]

---

[26] Sorry, I just couldn't think of anything clever for this chapter title. If only my book had fewer chapters!

Ideally, reading a book feels like hanging out with the person narrating it or the characters in it. This is the major job of the Voice. It's like the book's personality. Whether the book is funny or deep, whimsical or wise. Even funny books come in many different flavors: sly, hysterical, sarcastic…

SARCASTIC! SARCASTIC!

I VOTE FOR SARCASTIC!

WHY AM I NOT SURPRISED?

SARCASM IS FUN,

AND A LOT OF PEOPLE RESPOND TO IT.

BUT IT CAN BE KIND OF HARD TO SUSTAIN FOR TWO HUNDRED PAGES.

IT STARTS TO GET A LITTLE TIRESOME.

THATS WHY YOU HAVE TO BE CAREFUL ABOUT THE VOICE YOU CHOOSE FOR A LONGER PROJECT.

A TWEET IS ONE THING. A BOOK'S ANOTHER.

WOW. I NEVER THOUGHT ABOUT IT THAT WAY BEFORE. TALK ABOUT PRESSURE.

EXACTLY.

THE GOOD THING IS THERE'S A LOT OF ROOM TO PLAY.

JUST LOOK AT US:

WE'RE USING MULTIPLE VOICES IN YOUR BOOK.

THERE'S YOUNG RYAN,

WHO'S LIVING YOUR BOOK.

AND ADULT RYAN,

WHO'S NARRATING YOUR BOOK...

...AND HAVING A CONVERSATION WITH ME IN BETWEEN.

THAT WAS MY IDEA.

AND A GOOD ONE!

USING TWO VOICES HAS HELPED US TELL...

...A MORE COMPLETE STORY.

AND, I HOPE, HELPED US BE MORE NATURAL AND NOT TOO NARRATE-Y.

THAT'S A WORD, RIGHT, TOMLINSON?

• • •

"This is it," I whispered quietly.

I inched my way to the edge and looked over to see what looked like a mile-long fall onto solid concrete. I took one last look around to see all the gigantic titans stuffing their faces. I was reassured.

"This is not the world I want to live in."

I jumped straight up into the air and arched forward to the ground, just like a diver. "AAAAAHHHHHHH!" I screamed as I fell closer and closer to the ground, nearly inches away from impact—when suddenly one of the nearby gigantic titans shouted at me.

"Hey!" he yelled.

And just like that, everything ended. Back to reality.

I was down on my knees, holding my mom's VHS camera inches away from the ground of the restaurant I was in. I didn't even need to look up to know that the angry voice that had interrupted my filming belonged to my uncle Richie.

Picture a large, serious, and powerful-looking man with a full head of grayish-white hair and glasses that I believe may be permanently attached to his face. Think that old guy on the bucket of chicken, but without the beard, or jolliness, or smile, or really anything that has to do with being merry.

"Be quiet," he said sternly.

"But I was almost done!" I complained.

"With what?"

"The point of view of an ant. Y'know, how this restaurant would look if you were an ant."

Uncle Richie stared at me with his eyebrows arched. I was in the middle of deciphering if that meant he was angry or confused when one of his three daughters —my older cousin, Liza—hopped into our conversation, uninvited.

"You're so stupid, Ryan," Liza said, laughing.

This was November 2003. I was thirteen years old and in eighth grade. I was pretty used to people calling me stupid. I was at a family dinner at a Chinese restaurant. Not just my family family—my mom, my dad, and my brother, Kyle—but all hundred members of my extended family, gathered to celebrate my grandparents' fiftieth wedding anniversary, hosted by my mom and her brothers.

Of course, being that I was a teenager at an event like this, I was extremely bored. I looked around the room, listening in on the painfully clichéd small talk that family and family friends have when they haven't seen one another in more than a month. I scanned the room for something more interesting to engage in when I saw my mom in the corner of the restaurant, filming the party with her camcorder.

"Can I do that?" I asked, walking up to her with my hands extended, as if begging for her camera.

(Cue spotlight on video camera, and surge dramatic music, to make it clear that this was my BIG moment.)

My mom lowered her camcorder, looking at me suspiciously.

"You better actually film the party," she said.

"I know!" I shot back.

"This is important," she said, handing over the camcorder.

"I got it."

This was it. I finally had something interesting to occupy me. Not only that, but it was an important task that mattered to everyone here, and I was going to nail it. I got wide shots. Close-ups. Interviews. Everything was going smoothly.

Until…

I had an idea.

What if this party were seen from the perspective of an ant?

I set the camera down on a nearby table. The lens was pointed at a plate with a folded cloth napkin, which looked massive through the camcorder.

I hit Record.

"This is the life of an ant," I said in the fake dramatic tone of a voice-over.

Moving the camera over the tabletop, I came up to a dumpling.

"Ah, it's raining giant dumplings," I shrieked. "I'm going to be crushed alive."

I whipped the camera backward, as if the ant was rapidly reversing in hopes of saving his life. Charting a new course, I moved the camera across the length of the table, dodging obstacles and offering a play-by-play of the action.

Reaching the table's edge, I lowered the camera onto the floor and ran it over the carpeting. Whenever I came to an obstruction, I improvised a solution and a punch line to go with it. Eventually, one of those obstructions was my uncle Richie.

By the time I was done filming that night, I'd managed to achieve my first few minutes of pure comedy gold. I mean, we're talking Oscar, Emmy, Golden Globe, VMA, Tony, Grammy, and People's Choice Award. They were all destined to be mine.

What I had not gotten? Basically, the party video my mom had asked for.

Not that anyone in my family ever watched it. And neither did I.

But it didn't matter. Making that video hadn't been boring at all. It had been fun. It was the first thing I'd found that I was really excited about in a long time—the first thing I was maybe even good at. And man, I needed that.

Everything changed for me. Not because my bullies suddenly developed hearts of gold (they didn't) and we became besties (no thanks). And not because I finally made some real friends by my eighth-grade year, so I had kids to hang out with in school. But because I found a thing I loved—something that gave me all-new focus (pun intended).

It was like the video camera had flipped a switch in my mind, releasing all these jokes and ideas and images. What had I been doing every day for what felt like forever? Running and rerunning different scenarios in my head. I could come up with ideas all day. Sure, some of them were stupid, but that was okay. I could think of new ideas, and I did. Trying all of them out—good, bad, and ugly—was so much fun.

Finally, for the first time in my life, I was doing something not because I had to do it. It wasn't like school, or judo, or basketball with all the rules, and the drills, and the need to compete against others and try to be the best (or not try at all, when I wasn't any good). This was zero pressure. It was just something I enjoyed doing. It didn't matter that I wasn't particularly good at it at first. I did it because I wanted to. Lightbulb moment: *more of this!*

Having a video camera at my disposal was pretty much the definition of awesome. It transformed moments that normally would have been annoying into moments when I could at least make myself laugh. Maybe even get the upper hand.

Remember how bad I used to feel when I had to go to judo tournaments with my big brother, Kyle, and overhear people talk about how he was so much better than me? Well, when I went to watch Kyle face his judo opponent at a match in May 2004, I now watched through the lens of our family video camera.

And that meant now I had the power.

I zoomed WAY in on Kyle's face.

"He looks nervous," I narrated.

From there, I went on to make fun of both my big brother's and the referee's facial expressions. And my big brother's performance.

"He got lucky," I deadpanned after Kyle made yet another awesome move.

I could entertain myself and make reality less annoying (to me). It made judo (and Kyle) bearable (almost). Making it my new way of finally conquering two of the things I'd struggled with most as a kid: my big brother and boring judo. Make that three things: also the fact that my big brother was really good at judo, while I stunk.

●　●　●

Here's a reality check. Kyle and I haven't done judo in years, but that video still exists. If people watch it now, they're going to be seeing my version of reality. And even if they can tell I'm making things up for comic effect, that still means I'm the one who created the official, lasting record of what happened.

Funny and fake, or not.

●　●　●

Once I started summer vacation that year, I had even more time to make videos. I started rounding up my friends in the neighborhood to collaborate with me. We filmed whenever we were all bored (which was pretty much all the time). I still had basketball and judo practice, but I wasn't into swimming or surfing or fishing, like other kids from our town. So that left quite a bit of free time. And I wasn't the only one looking for something to do either. Whoever was around became my impromptu cast and crew. I still shot videos by myself sometimes, but it was much more fun with others. My videos became longer and more intricate. And I loved making people laugh.

Have you ever heard the stories about how Quentin Tarantino got started?[27] While he was writing his first scripts, he worked as a video-store clerk for five years,

---

[27] Me neither. But Tomlinson told me about them.

living and breathing movies. All he wanted to do was watch movies, and talk about movies, and make movies. And so he did.

I was like that after I got my first taste of making videos. Any free time now had a greater purpose. I picked up my family's camcorder whenever I could, setting out to make a short video nearly every week. It didn't matter how bad I was at it, or how stupid my ideas were. I was having too much fun to care.

I learned by doing, playing with our video camera, goofing around, making mistakes. When I stumbled on a cool effect or a funny joke, it was usually just that—something I'd accidentally happened on, more than something I'd planned because I knew it would have a certain impact. But when I played back the video, I always had a hunch when something was good. At least I knew when it made me laugh. And that was my powerful takeaway from my miserable middle-school days: *Go for the laugh.* It's the secret sauce that catches people's attention and makes them respond.

Each video I made helped me get better and think of new ideas. They were just a bunch of silly skits, but it was my start. I also learned by studying the masters. When I started messing around with a video camera, all my favorite movies came back to me as inspiration, and they gave me a new scheme: *I could re-create stuff.*

Now that I had enough people for a whole production, I got really into doing spoofs of my favorite movies and TV shows.

A spoof of *Pimp My Ride.*

A spoof of *The Grudge.*

A spoof of *Blair Witch Project.*

A spoof of *Kill Bill.*

A spoof of *The Fast and the Furious.*

A spoof of pretty much all my favorite films—my first one was *Napoleon*

Dynamite. I loved *Zoolander*, but I didn't touch it, because, really, how was I going to make that comic masterpiece any funnier than it already was?

I could spend hours on my videos without even realizing how much time had gone by. Or caring about how good the final product was. Sure, I didn't want them to suck. But I didn't get discouraged when a video wasn't as good as I'd envisioned. I just tried to make the next one better.

Good thing I didn't get too down on myself. My technique was amateurish at best, as was my equipment. My costumes—well, to even use the word *costume* is a stretch. We didn't buy any props or costumes; we just made do with whatever we had around the house. We didn't have a prop gun, so we used an old Nerf gun that was lying around. We didn't have legit costumes to act out Harry Potter, so we used an old faded-blue bedsheet. It was obviously a sheet, and that haphazard, homemade quality added to the comedy. (I hope.)

Occasionally, my lack of creativity or editing ability led to accidental hilarity. Sometimes a scene would start, and it would have three failed intros that you'd be able to see really quickly, like a half second of each of the previous bad takes. It led to this awkward, almost stop-motion, blooper-reel feel that was genuinely funny. Even when it wasn't, that was the best I could manage, so I made do.

● ● ●

Believe it or not, that kind of guerrilla, DIY-style filmmaking that I had no choice but to do in the beginning has actually influenced what I do today, even though I've obviously got a few more tricks and techniques to work with now. I actually *like* it when the seams show a little. And some of my favorite types of jokes are when I'm breaking the fourth wall.

THAT'S A FANCY TERM FOR TALKING INTO THE CAMERA,

AS IF YOU'RE DIRECTLY ADDRESSING THE AUDIENCE.

LIKE I'M DOING RIGHT NOW.

HEY, YOU.

YEAH,

YOU.

HEY, WHAT?

NOT TALKING TO YOU.

SHOULD I BE WORRIED ABOUT YOU?

YOU'RE ALREADY TALKING TO ONE GHOST.

NOW YOU'RE TALKING TO ANOTHER?

NO, I'M TALKING TO THE READER.

OH, OKAY.

When I do this, it's almost like I really *am* talking to you. I actually think that's what YouTube has over all the other mediums. We're able to have that kind of direct connection with our viewers. And make those kinds of obvious, silly jokes right to you, without worrying that we're going to ruin the effect, or the story, if we don't follow the rules.

We can break *all* the rules.

Because there are *no* rules.

WHAT?

THEN WHY WASTE TIME LEARNING THEM?!

IT'S NOT WASTING TIME.

THAT'S WHAT I'M TRYING TO TELL YOU.

WHETHER WE'RE TALKING ABOUT WRITING A BOOK OR MAKING A VIDEO OR ALMOST ANYTHING CREATIVE,

YOU'RE GOING TO ENCOUNTER RULES THAT HELP YOU THROUGH THE PROCESS,

AND THE BETTER YOU GET AT WRITING/VIDEOING/ WHATEVERING...

...THE MORE YOU ARE ABLE TO TEST THE RULES

AND GO YOUR OWN CREATIVE WAY.

WHOA

THAT'S DEEP.

Every hero has to be motivated by a clear desire for something really, really important. Something he wants so much that he'll go to any length to achieve it. He'll fight dragons. He'll trek through snowy mountains with only a single match to keep himself warm. He'll get up and go to school every day, no matter how badly he's being bullied.

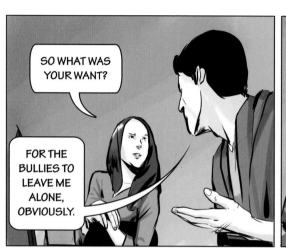

SO WHAT WAS YOUR WANT?

FOR THE BULLIES TO LEAVE ME ALONE, OBVIOUSLY.

THAT'S A GIVEN, BUT WAS THERE SOMETHING YOU WANTED THAT YOU THOUGHT WOULD SOLVE ALL YOUR PROBLEMS?

HIGH SCHOOL!

BANG!

OH, THANKS.

BUT YEAH, I HAD TO ENDURE YEAR AFTER YEAR OF BAD STUFF. AND ALL I WANTED WAS... HIGH SCHOOL.

REALLY?! OH, SORRY.

YOU KNEW? WHY DIDN'T YOU WARN ME?

I HADN'T EVEN MET YOU BACK THEN.

OKAY, GOOD POINT. I'LL LET THIS ONE SLIDE.

I think it's important to be as specific as possible here. Now, when I say that Young Ryan was finally getting what he'd wanted all along, I don't really mean that he wanted to go to high school. I mean that he wanted to be reunited with his friends from elementary school. Because he just knew that once this happened, his life was going to get a million times better!

• • •

Well, that thought lasted for about five minutes on my first day of my freshman year. Here's the thing about high school. Or at least my high school.[28] They run on one thing: cliques.

So that meant, from day one, I had to find out where I belonged.[29]

At our school, this played out in the quad, a big area of grass, bordered by covered walkways and surrounded by the cafeteria and classroom buildings, where all the kids hung out at lunch and between periods. Or as I soon came to think of it:

No-man's-land.

In one area, we had all varieties of jocks. The big football players, who always wore their jerseys to school. The perky cheerleaders, who hung on them. Next to them, but not exactly with them, the baseball players. And next to them, although I didn't know who they were at the time, the wrestling group.

Then you had the druggies, a bunch of big girls who were really *moke*,[30] the goth/emo-looking kids who wore all black and had nose rings and dyed hair, and finally, the nerdier, overachiever kids who were very involved with extracurricular activities and had a lot of school spirit.

It only took me one trip out to the quad on my first day of school to survey the scene and see that I didn't belong in any of these groups.

Sure, I'd tested well at my last school, and they'd told me I was smart. And I

---

[28] And pretty much every high school I've ever seen in a movie, TV show, or nightmare (I've had plenty).

[29] I think I would have rather battled a dragon.

[30] That's kind of like Hawaii teen slang for people you think of when the "Bad Boys" song plays—they don't care about schoolwork and are ready and willing to fight with anyone.

did my homework like I was supposed to. But I'd definitely learned the lesson about not acting *too* smart and getting singled out for abuse. And it's not like caring about school automatically made me a nerd. Not that there's anything wrong with being a nerd, of course. It almost would have been easier if I'd identified with those kids, because then at least I would've had a crowd to call my own.

I still did judo and was planning to play basketball in the winter. But in no way did I think of myself as a jock.

And I wasn't one of the kids who drank and smoked pot on the weekend. So the druggies weren't my people either.

I was just me.

There didn't seem to be a group of people who went by the label "just me," and since it seemed like high school was all about labeling people and keeping them in their groups, I didn't feel like I belonged anywhere.

I slunk into the school building and made my way to my next class, even though it didn't start for an hour. Without anyone to back me up, I certainly wasn't going to walk across the quad by myself. At least when I was standing outside my classroom, it looked like I had somewhere to be. And it wasn't as obvious that I didn't have anyone to be there with.

Because, oh, by the way, those old friends from elementary school I'd been looking forward to reuniting with?

Duh. They had also gone to another school for the past three years. Where they'd made new friends. Sure, they smiled and nodded at me in the halls, but that was about it. Once again, I was on my own.

Also during my first day, I saw a beam of light at the far end of the hallway: Nicole.

And just as quickly, her radiant glimmer was eclipsed by a heavy shadow: her boyfriend. Immediately, I didn't like the guy. He looked like the guys who had bullied me in middle school—dressed in the kind of slouchy board shorts and T-shirt that gave them the general air of surfers, whether or not they surfed. I couldn't figure out why she would want to date a guy like that, other than maybe that he was "cool." And together, they were part of a clique of cool kids.

They had cool-kid clothes, and cool-kid hair, and they had this almost rebellious attitude that was cool too. They did things I would never do, like show up late to class, or leave school and go to the beach.

Damn, I should do that once, just to show I'm not a nerd, I thought.

But I never did. I didn't want to get in trouble. And I didn't have anyone to go to the beach with anyhow.

But I was nothing if not persistent: I continued to have a crush on Nicole, and she continued to not notice me.

As the year progressed, I was bummed to see that high school wasn't that different from middle school. It didn't help that I think I seriously had PTSD from my last school. That's that condition where you go through something so bad that you have a hard time believing life will ever be good again. At school, I was always on edge. The memory of the humiliation and frustration I'd felt so often courtesy of Dick and his minions was like a weight I was always carrying around. I didn't want to be that loser ever again, so I didn't leave any openings for it to happen.

I planned every minute of my day. Basically, my approach to school was guided by one goal: *Try not to get noticed, in order to try not to get bullied.* It mostly worked, and my existence wasn't as bad as it had been in middle school, but I wasn't exactly living the high life. I pretty much lived for the weekends, when I could shoot videos with my neighborhood friends.

●　　●　　●

SO I TAKE IT THAT HIGH SCHOOL WASN'T YOUR TRUE WANT ANYMORE?

NOT EVEN CLOSE. BECAUSE WHAT I WANTED WASN'T REALLY WHAT I NEEDED.

WHAT I ACTUALLY NEEDED WAS TO FIND THINGS I LIKED TO DO,

AND PEOPLE WHO WERE MY PEOPLE, WHO LIKED ME FOR WHO I WAS.

WOW, THAT'S PRETTY INSPIRING.

BUT NOT TOO NARRATE-Y, RIGHT?

RYAN, YOU'RE KILLING ME.

I KNOW YOU'RE PROBABLY JEALOUS BECAUSE YOU'VE NEVER INVENTED A WORD BEFORE.

SOMETHING LIKE THAT. OKAY, TELL ME ABOUT YOUR TRUE WANT.

A few months into the school year, it was time for me to sign up for my winter sport.

I had been planning to try out for the basketball team. Even though I wasn't exactly a natural, that's just what I'd always played. But one Sunday night the previous spring, toward the end of eighth grade, I'd been sitting with my dad and one of my uncles at our usual family dinner and that all changed.

"How's school going, Ryan?" Uncle Winna asked me.

"Fine," I lied.

"Are you going to play basketball next year in high school?" he asked.

"Yeah, probably. That's always been my team sport."

"Maybe you should try wrestling instead," he offered.

"That's a great idea," my dad said. "Uncle Winna was a good wrestler in high school and can give you some pointers."

"Don't get pinned," my uncle joked. "Yeah, sure, I'll work with you."

I knew my uncle had wrestled in high school and medaled and that he taught wrestling, so he probably knew what he was talking about. But I wasn't so sure.

"I don't know," I said. "Won't I have to wear spandex?"

No way! I thought. *That's not gonna happen.*

"Nah, the uniforms aren't spandex," my uncle said.

"Are you sure?" I asked.

"Yeah, you don't have to wear spandex if you don't want to," he said.

"See, Ryan, no spandex," my dad said. "You should try it."

It seemed like they were giving each other a knowing, amused laugh. But I figured I was probably just imagining things.

Maybe I'll actually be good at wrestling, I thought. *Because I'm definitely not good at basketball. At least I have a judo background, which could help me on the mat.*

• • •

Okay, let's leave little eighth-grade Ryan right there, daydreaming about his glorious spandex-free future on the wrestling mat, and meet up with ninth-grade Ryan...on the wrestling mat...contemplating the spandex in his immediate future.[31]

• • •

It was my first day of practice, and the coaches had everyone line up. They started

---

[31] Yes, I talked to my dad and my uncle about it later, and they both remember straight-up lying to me about what the uniforms were made of. Adults: You just can't trust 'em.

teaching us the warm-ups we'd do at the beginning of each practice. Most of the other guys were watching closely, trying to follow what the coaches were doing. But these were basically the same warm-ups I'd been doing at judo since I was five years old. *No problem.* When they showed us how to do some moves, some of the guys looked awkward and off balance, but it felt natural for me because of judo. For once, I wasn't the one kid having trouble following the coach's instructions, the one who was totally lost and always getting in trouble because of it.

"Nice job, Ryan," one of the coaches said.

What was this feeling? Getting affirmation, instead of being criticized? It felt... good?

And that wasn't all.

My judo background made a big difference. So did my basketball background, actually.

Halfway through our first practice, my new teammates were slowing down. Some of them even had to stop right where they were and bend over and rest their elbows on their knees, trying to catch their breath and not puke. Even though it was the first day of the season, I was already in good shape because I'd been doing multiple sports for most of my life.

For once, I wasn't the worst at something. And I actually started to feel confident during practice. I was even having fun.

By the time I had a match and had to wear spandex for the first time, I'd become such a different, more confident person that I couldn't have cared less. Spandex was just the uniform. And it was the last thing on my mind.

I was there to wrestle.

And to win.

I loved it.

And finally, I had a place to hang out in the quad during lunch.

GO AHEAD AND LAUGH, BUT SOMETIMES IT'S THE LITTLE THINGS THAT ARE THE MOST IMPORTANT.

I'M NOT LAUGHING.

SNIFF

ARE YOU... CRYING?

I'M JUST SO HAPPY TO HEAR YOU SAY YOU LOVED SOMETHING AT SCHOOL.

UM, LET'S JUST GET BACK TO THE STORY.

READY WHEN YOU ARE.

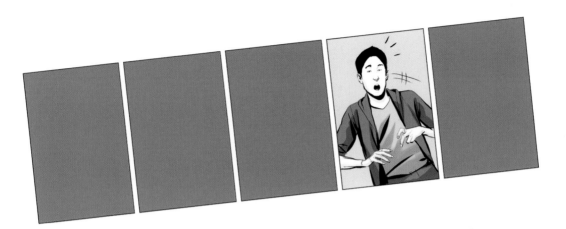

It ain't easy being a hero in a story. Just when it seems like everything is finally going your way—after plenty of wanting, and working, and wanting some more—there's usually one final catch. You know, this is the part of the movie where the kidnappers have been paid the ransom, and the hostage has been set free, and then someone double-crosses someone else, and there's one more heart-in-your-throat chase scene before the final resolution and happily ever after.

Wrestling was going great. There was just one catch.

I may have had a place to hang out at lunch now, but finding my place on the team wasn't easy.

I won't bore you with all the details, but basically I had to drop sixteen pounds. As soon as I possibly could. Definitely before the next match. Because the only weight class I could compete in was 103—and I weighed 119 pounds.[32]

Part of me wanted to just throw in the towel and walk away. *Couldn't something just go my way for once?* But another part of me wanted so badly to compete on this team that I wouldn't let anything stand in my way.

That part won.

I brought my usual logical approach to the problem, and I lost a few pounds by cutting out desserts and snacks.

But then I plateaued. Eventually I was limiting myself to a can of tuna a day. And very little water. While subjecting myself to more and more grueling workouts. I was so close. But I still had a few more pounds to lose before our next meet.

The older guys on the team had been doing this for several years now, and they were pros at cutting weight. Fast. So I started observing them closely and learning all their tricks.

We were spending a lot of time together—at practice and at workouts in between—and before I knew it, I had a new group of friends. It's not like we were instantly tight, but they were the first people at school who'd really accepted me. It had been such a rough few years. Finally, I'd found something I liked to do and was getting good at, and it came with a whole group of potential friends. I'd found the people I fit in with.

[32] My actual weight class was already taken by a sophomore. Damn that guy.

A couple of weeks before the match, a few of us were in the locker room after practice.

"Good workout today, Ryan," one of my older teammates said as I stepped off the scale, disappointed that I still had seven pounds to go.

"Thanks," I said. *Seven pounds?* It felt impossible. I couldn't possibly eat less or exercise more. I had been working so hard.

"What are you at these days?"

"One ten."

"Yeah, those last few pounds are always the hardest. Why don't you try taking some of these?"

He held out a plastic bottle. I nodded like I knew exactly what it was he was offering me, like it was no big deal. When really it was a *big* deal. We weren't supposed to take diuretics or weight-loss supplements. Our coaches would kill us if they knew. But this was one of the best wrestlers on the team offering to help me work harder and be better too. What could be wrong with that?

"Thanks, man," I said, holding out my hand for him to shake a dozen of the pills into my palm.

That's how it started.

The pills were a miracle. They provided extra energy, curbed my hunger, and burned fat. Everything a wrestler could want. I started taking them all the time. And they were working. I was almost down to 103. But I wasn't quite there. *So close.* I just had to work a little harder. Push a little harder.

The highest recommended dose was three pills. One day after school, as the upcoming match loomed and my weight still wasn't where it needed to be, I started to worry that I wasn't going to make it. I only had a few more pounds to go, so I took nine pills. And then I did what I did every day before wrestling practice started: I went to run five miles. As usual, I'd eaten almost nothing that day—only half a can of tuna—and I'd had only a few small sips of water. I was wearing my heaviest sweats. I hoped the pills would help me sweat as much as possible and drop the final weight I needed to lose. The weigh-in was two days away.

I started running laps with a few of my teammates. And here's how that went for me:

The guys were talking about a girl they both thought was cute, and I was trying to figure out what lap we were on. My vision was getting all swimmy and going black around the edges. I was having trouble holding a single thought…

Hey, what was I thinking just then?

I don't remember exactly what happened next.

I was running.

I was falling.

I was waking up, lying on the ground.

My teammate Logan was standing over me. "Dude. Are you okay?"

"I don't know."

He bent down. "What are you doing?" he asked.

"I don't know. I think I passed out."

He laughed as he helped me up and walked with me to get water. As out of it as I was, I couldn't help but note that he hadn't made fun of me or called me stupid for fainting. As miserable as I felt in that moment, I also felt a tiny bubble of excitement.[33] Even though I'd been hanging out with these guys for a few weeks now, I still hadn't totally let go of the fear that they'd decide I was lame. But I was part of a team, and for the first time I really felt like I belonged. After I drank the smallest amount of water possible, we went to practice, like nothing had happened.

[33] Yes! I knew I'd find another place for that bubble of excitement.

Full disclosure: That was the first time I passed out, but it wasn't the last. And I wasn't the only one on the team it happened to. Nearly passing out or blacking out completely became so common for us that we had our own joke about it. Whenever one of us was close to going unconscious, he'd start to see these little black spots at the edges of his vision. "Our friends are back," he'd joke. Laughing got us through.

Instead of being miserable because of all this deprivation and the extra workouts and the sore muscles, I'd never felt better in my life. Looking back, I realize what was happening: Like with my videos, I'd finally found something I cared about enough to really push myself. All those years I was rolling my eyes at my coaches and Senseis who'd yelled at me when I was younger—that's because I wasn't inspired by judo or basketball. It's *totally* different when you find something you like and push yourself, because that's when you learn what you can accomplish, and you start to see yourself differently.

Everyone on my team was so tough, and they were always impressing me by doing the impossible. So I started wanting to do the impossible too. Soon enough, I was.[34] I was doing so many things I'd never thought possible before, and it made me realize that I could push myself to do anything I wanted, on the mat and off.

[34] If you had told Young Ryan that he'd spend his high-school afternoons running five miles, then going to wrestling practice, then running a couple more miles afterward...he would've laughed his head off, because Young Ryan could not even run a mile.

• • •

Finally, it was time for my meet. My weight was hovering right at 103 pounds. I just had to keep it there long enough to wrestle for my team. When we arrived at the gym in the morning, my teammates and I weighed in. As I climbed onto the scale, I took a deep breath and let it out, then looked at the number as the official said it.

"One oh two."

A whole pound under my weight class. Another **MOMENTOUS MOMENT** in my life when I didn't feel like a loser.

I won my match that day. And I won several more that season. Everything began to turn around, first on the mat, and then off.

But the funny thing was, winning almost didn't matter. Of course, I'd worked hard, and victory was the best possible reward. But what felt even more important was what I'd proved to myself: *When I really care about something and put in the effort, I can do anything.* That made me feel more confident than I ever had before.

Here's the crazy part too. Talk about the ultimate dose of perspective—when you're starving, and agonizing over how dehydrated you are, it brings your focus in super close. When you're that dedicated to your purpose, and you're at that point of weakness—every time you stand up, you feel lightheaded, and you walk to the bathroom and you're exhausted, and you brush your teeth and your arm feels like lead, it's so tired, and you rinse your mouth but you can't drink any of that water—nothing else matters. Literally. If someone made fun of me during that time, I didn't care. I was at the point of survival. It made me get my priorities straight, fast. And it was hard to ever care again about things like popularity or cliques.

I had a purpose. And that made me strong. And I had true friends. Just when it didn't matter so much to me anymore, I had people to eat lunch with (of course, ironically, none of us could actually eat lunch, so I guess you could say that I had people with whom I could watch the non-wrestlers eat lunch). And to hang out with in the quad. (That *was* nice.)

WE **ARE** ALMOST DONE, AREN'T WE? SO, YEAH, I GUESS SO.

I HAD TRANSFORMED MYSELF AND—MORE IMPORTANTLY—HOW I THOUGHT ABOUT MYSELF.

AGAIN?!

SORRY.

OKAY, CAN WE GET BACK TO IT?

THERE'S MORE?!

Since I had to learn what a prologue is, I went ahead and learned what an epilogue is too.[35] It's basically a chapter at the end of the book that's not really a part of the main story, where you can reflect on what was in the book or give a little more info about how things turned out.

YOU DON'T HAVE TO DO AN EPILOGUE, YOU KNOW...

I KNOW, BUT IT FELT WEIRD TO WRITE A BOOK ABOUT WHEN I WAS YOUNGER

AND NOT EVEN MENTION YOUTUBE, SINCE IT BASICALLY CHANGED MY LIFE AGAIN.

[35] There I go pushing myself again. I didn't have to learn what an epilogue is. I could've just written "the end."

Right at the end of my freshman year, when life was feeling better all around, I discovered this new little website called YouTube. You might have heard of it.

This was back in the early days of YouTube, and there wasn't much up there (unless you like funny videos of cats, and who doesn't?!), but I thought it was pretty cool. There were some people—some of them kids like me—making and posting videos. It was sort of like discovering there was this whole community of people out there who were also making videos to show their grandparents at Sunday night dinner. Except they were posting them online for non-grandparents to watch. Seeing what other people were up to gave me even more ideas for my own videos. And it was a great place to post my videos so my friends could watch them.

I was still doing all my filming with our family's camcorder, though, which recorded onto VHS tapes to be played in (that most ancient of artifacts) a VCR.

Which meant there was no way for me to easily post my videos online. Naturally, I used the Tri-Beam Offensive to eventually convince my parents to get a digital camera, so I could upload videos directly to YouTube. Now if I wanted someone to watch my video, I didn't have to carry it over to their house or wait for them to come to mine. This also meant I could finally edit my videos with a technique slightly more sophisticated than the rewind button.

I now had lots of friends. Most of them were my teammates from the wrestling team, and some became regulars in my videos.

Another trivia fact: In my early videos with these guys, we called ourselves the Yabo Crew. Those videos got flagged for having *copyrighted music* (I had no idea what that was at the time), so most of those videos got taken down from my You-Tube channel.

Cut to: July 20, 2006. You'll for sure remember that was the date when I first created my nigahiga YouTube account—since it's a national holiday now, and there are big parades in every major city, plus the sparkly fireworks, and everyone has the day off from work.[36]

It was summer vacation between my sophomore and junior years of high school, so I had more free time than during the school year. My days all looked a little something like this: Wake up, look at the clock. If it's before noon, go back to sleep because it's too early to get up. If not, get up, brush my teeth, change my clothes (sometimes not), go to the refrigerator, and grab a Lunchable or a Hot Pocket. Stare lovingly at it. Just kidding—of course I'd eat it in about two seconds flat. Then play some video games. Eventually, realize it's dark outside and head to the Starbucks parking lot with a friend who could drive, or just drive around town and waste gas. It was a wild life I was living.

[36] Not really. (Not yet.)

On this particular Thursday, I did wake up before noon, and although I tried going back to sleep, I couldn't. So there I was, awake and out of bed in the ten o'clock hour—it was eerie. After I grabbed a Hot Pocket, I went to settle in at my computer for a longer-than-usual video-game session. I was not going to waste these extra hours. But when I turned on the monitor, it was on the YouTube home page. I didn't remember being on YouTube the night before. Weird! I was about to minimize the window when it seemed like the Sign Up tab started to blink. I'd never seen it do that before. It's like it was begging me to click on it. So of course I clicked on it. And when I did, the lights in my room dimmed for a second and then got really bright, and I just knew that I had to start my own YouTube channel.

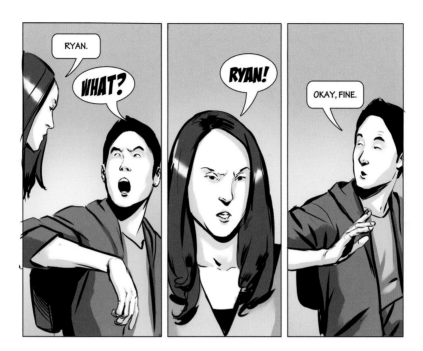

JK. None of that happened. I don't know why I decided to finally start a YouTube channel that day. But aren't you glad I did? I am.

• • •

I was learning to figure out a lot of things for myself around this time and feeling more confident because of it. And I'm not just talking about videos. Like how I'd managed to figure out the best way to handle my bullies' impact in middle school. And how I'd pushed my limits when I'd joined the wrestling team and discovered I had so much more drive than I'd ever known. I'd learned to make life better for myself by changing my perspective and working hard to achieve my goals. As I got older, the stakes felt higher because I had to start thinking about my future.

I'd been volunteering at our island's main hospital, in the pharmacy and in the radiology department, and considered being a radiologist for my career. Until I found out that I'd have to go to med school. No way.[37] And I'd thought about being a pharmacist for a while. But volunteering in that department was the most boring thing ever. So I crossed that off my list too. I was better at figuring out what I *didn't* want to do than at finding a possible future life that would make me happy. But through it all, I loved making videos, and it was clear that wouldn't change.

I feel like some people have the idea that those of us who make YouTube videos sit at home all day watching our numbers creep up, one by one.

Maybe some people are doing that.

But not me.

There has never been a time when I've hoped for a specific number of viewers. Instead, I've always just wanted to blow people's minds with each video I've made. And as far as numbers go, I've always set my expectations low and then been pleasantly surprised when a video did well. I've found that this is the best way to avoid being disappointed: Lowball yourself in life, and you'll be fine.

I tested out this approach in other areas of my life too.

At the state championship wrestling match during my senior year, I was sitting next to my coach. We both knew how hard I'd worked—and how far I'd come—during the past four years and that this was my last chance to compete for my high-school team.

"This is such a big moment, Ryan," Coach said. "I'm really proud of you."

"Thanks," I said. "Yeah, it is big, I guess."

But what I was really thinking was: *I'm gonna get second place, and it will be awesome.*

[37] I may have been all about changing my perspective and pushing myself for my goals, but I also knew my limits.

And then when I won first, the victory was even better. But if I had won second, I would have been okay, because I'd prepared myself for that outcome.

I know the cool, mature thing is to say that winning doesn't matter. To say that it's how you play the game.

And, of course, there's a part of that logic that's total crap.

We all want to win. It's human nature.

But there's also some truth to the fact that winning isn't everything. If you set realistic expectations for yourself and you know you've done your best to get there, then there really is satisfaction in how you played the game. And this can apply to anything—making videos, wrestling, judo, basketball…writing a book.

Just picture me on the mat at the end of my senior year, earning my state championship. And think about how, six years earlier, I used to lie awake every night (or is it lay awake? I never know) imagining I was going to kill myself, because I felt so miserable and powerless and alone. And here I was now, a winner, with teammates, friends, a girlfriend,[38] and even fans in the audience. I'd started getting recognized by people I didn't know on the street because of my YouTube videos, pretty much as soon as I began uploading them. Which was awesome. And weird.

I had done all that for myself. If I could do all that, I could do anything I set my mind to.

It didn't really matter if I won. (But it was nice when I did.)

●　　●　　●

So, that's my story. I hope you liked it, or learned something from it, or at the very least, finished it. I did write it for you, even though TPC seems to think I wrote it for them.…

---

[38] Not Nicole. I found someone who was way better for me and prettier.

THANKS, TOMLINSON. BUT AREN'T YOU SAD THAT YOU'RE NOT GOING TO GET CREDIT FOR ANY OF THIS?

I MEAN, YOU DID THE WORK TOO.

NAH, I'M USED TO IT.

I'M A GHOSTWRITER. THAT'S WHAT WE DO.

SO... I GUESS THIS IS IT.

WHERE WE SAY GOOD-BYE?

THIS PART IS NEVER EASY. WE'VE BEEN THROUGH A LOT TOGETHER.

WE HAVE. I THINK I'M GOING TO...

MISS YOU?

I KNOW, KID. I'M CHARMING LIKE THAT. I'LL MISS YOU TOO.

THANKS FOR SHARING YOUR STORY WITH ME.

YOU KNOW WHERE TO FIND ME IF YOU WANT TO DO A SEQUEL.

SORRY, TPC...

WE WERE JUST NEVER GONNA AGREE ON SOME THINGS. AND IT IS MY NAME (AND FACE) ON THE COVER.

SO, JUST GONNA MAKE A **FEW** CHANGES BEFORE IT GOES TO THE PRINTER....

NOW YOU'LL GET THE STORY MY WAY, WITH THE BEHIND-THE-SCENES ACTION AND EVERYTHING.

TEEHEE